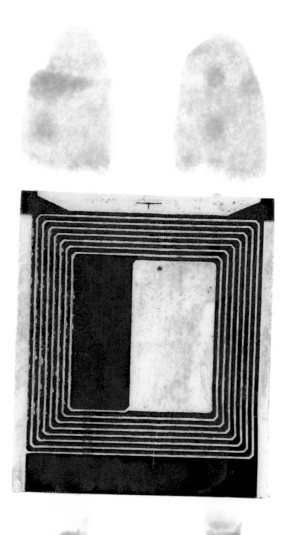

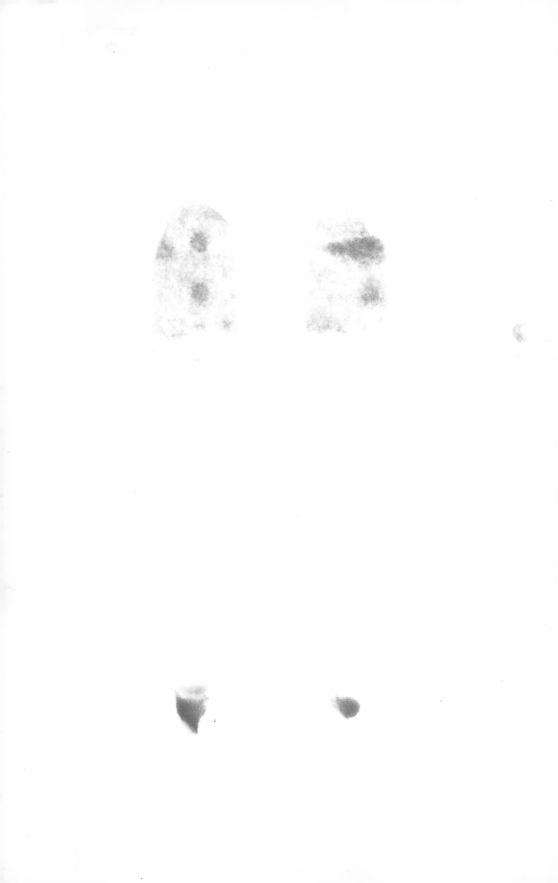

Walking is man's best medicine.
                              —HIPPOCRATES

RACEWALK TO FITNESS

The *Sensible* Alternative to Jogging and Running

HOWARD JACOBSON

SIMON AND SCHUSTER

NEW YORK

Published by Simon and Schuster
A Division of Gulf & Western Corporation
Simon & Schuster Building
Rockefeller Center
1230 Avenue of the Americas
New York, New York 10020

SIMON AND SCHUSTER and colophon
are trademarks of Simon & Schuster

Designed by Stanley S. Drate

Manufactured in the United States of America

1 2 3 4 5 6 7 8 9 10

Library of Congress Cataloging in Publication Data

Jacobson, Howard, date.
   Racewalk to fitness.

   1.   Walking (Sports)   2.   Physical fitness.
I.   Title.
GV1071.J3   796.5′1   80-10258
ISBN 0-671-24938-X

Acknowledgments

Special thanks to Rachel Carr and Ed Kimball for their guidance and many hours of assistance. Also to Mary Cunnane, my walking protégé, who "coached" me through much of this book.

Deep appreciation to my editor, Peter Schwed, who had confidence in me and my book.

I will always cherish my associations with the many people who helped and encouraged me through the years: Joe Yancey, Emil Von Elling, Joe Healy, Larry Ellis, Roy Chernock, Gordon McKenzie, Bruce MacDonald, Ron Daniel.

Thanks to Steve Hayden, Gary Westerfield, Larry Newman, and John Markon, for the unique coach-athlete-teammate relationship at the Long Island Athletic Club. To Olympians Shaul Ladany, Dave Romansky, and Todd Scully, for the opportunity to work with them.

Thanks to Judy Litchfield for the long hours of typing to meet my deadlines.

Sincere thanks to Stuart Pollack, the Struhls, the Barkins, the Ebers, and the Surreys for understanding me. And to Vin Salamone for easing my occasional aches and pains.

Special thanks to my friend, teammate, assistant director of the racewalking clinics—my son, Alan.

Finally, many thanks to my mother, Ruth, and to my ex-wife, Ora, for leaving dinner warming on the stove for so many years while I was out training.

PHOTOGRAPHIC CREDITS

Cover: Chloe Foote

Instructional: Rachel Carr and Ed Kimball, and Chloe Foote

Racing Photos: Elliott Denman and the Asbury Park Press

Others: Blue Cross and Blue Shield of America; Wide World Photos; United Press International; Editorial Photo Archives; Eli Attar; Andy Novick; David Jacobson; Gus Krug.

Models for pages 69–99: Grazia Dei and Howard Jacobson

This book is dedicated to Henry Laskau, who got me started in the sport of racewalking; and to my children, Alan, David, Karen and Lisa, whose cheers and encouragement have kept me going for so many years.

Contents

TWO

HERE'S HOW

THREE

THE ATHLETIC LIFE

FOUR

RACEWALKING'S WORLD

INTRODUCTION

You Don't Have to *Race* . . . to Racewalk

It's the *style* that counts . . . proper racewalk style promotes a high degree of fitness, even if you're not out to set records.

Racewalking is an Olympic sport, but it has suffered some years of undeserved decline in popularity. Now it has suddenly reversed and is coming back strongly, with even greater attention than ever before. Today the interest is particularly high because of the exercise benefits. The lure of competition still exists with one more new dimension added—women are now participating right along with the men.

The great thing about racewalking is that it's for everyone—children, adults and senior citizens alike—allowing all to get the most out of their bodies and enjoy life at the same time.

Running and racewalking have done so much for me during the past 35 years that I want to share my knowledge and experiences with every person interested in his or her own well-being. I have had a "running" (and walking) love affair with my sport since I started as a 15-year-old sophomore in high school. This love and its importance in my life have at times caused me to be accused of forsaking my family, business, friends, etc., to the point of obsession. I love to run. I love to racewalk. I love to compete and I love to coach. If obsession is defined as abnormal preoccupation with an idea, then I question that by asking: By whose standards is it abnormal? By those who are 20 or 30 pounds overweight? By those parents whose children—along with my own—were taught basketball, football and baseball by me because the parents were not able or not so inclined?

By those who have never been on an organized team and will never know about the camaraderie of athletics? What about the dreams of a ballet dancer? The burning passion of a painter? I am strong when I attack that hill, free when I run through the woods. I love it when I see my protégé improving—advancing with my help, his guts, my guts, his creativity, my creativity, his strength, my inspiration. We are both doing it together. There is no feeling like it. What do they know about dedication, creativity, pain, love? People like Bill Rodgers or Ron Laird or Nina Kuscsik know about dedication. My life-long friend and former teammate at New York University, Roy Chernock, now coaching track and cross-country at William and Mary College, once said to me when I was helping him coach his distance runners at C. W. Post College back in 1965: "Jake, you missed your calling. You should have been a full-time track coach." He knew.

I got my first head coaching responsibility after 22 years as a competitive runner and racewalker. I was asked to build a racewalking team for the Long Island Athletic Club. Coaching the team from 1966–1976 was the most rewarding experience of my entire life. As coach to some of the finest people and best athletes I have ever known, I had the opportunity to develop these men in a capacity that few coaches in this world ever have. Not only was I their coach, I was their teammate. I was still approaching my prime as a competitive racewalker at an age when most coaches had long since "hung up their shoes." When I "cracked the whip," I cracked it on myself as well.

Those were beautiful years coaching athletes to national and international teams, including the ultimate goal—the United States Olympic Racewalking Team. They will always stay with me. After my youngest son went away to college, I moved to New York City to avoid the hassle of commuting which I had done for so many years. That 3-hour saving gave me time for more training in the morning and for other interests after work. Because of my interest in hatha-yoga, which deals with the physical-training aspect of yoga, I tuned in even further to my body. As a trained athlete and coach, I had studied anatomy, kinesiology, nutrition and sportsmedicine and had a high degree of body awareness. With yoga and its emphasis on deep controlled breathing, I learned even more about my body and what I could do with it. I also tried altering my diet. At first I cut out all red meat. It has been 4 years now and I don't miss it a bit. I turned to vegetables, cheeses and fruits, and only occasionally to chicken or fish. About 2 years ago something drastic happened to my performance times—they reverted to those of 10 and 20 years previously. I feel like a kid. I love racing against younger people and finishing high up in the standings. Even if I don't win, I win. Everything seems to have come together. I have more energy. Somehow, I feel cleaner, stronger. My body has more flexibility, more stamina. I sleep like a baby. My weight is what it was in high school. After training in the park and having been besieged with questions about running and racewalking, injuries and training, it came to me that I must become a physical fitness consultant and share what I've experienced.

Now I am coach to many men and women who, like you, are interested in conditioning their bodies. My Racewalking Program eases people into a regimen of physical fitness with particular emphasis on the exercise of the future—*Racewalking.* Integrated into the program are yoga-based warm-up exercises which I call *Prekinetics,* designed to increase your flexibility for a better range of motion.

You are out of shape. You have been inactive for years. The Racewalking Program will start you into training by doing first things first and not put the jog before the walk. In order to prepare your cardio-respiratory and musculoskeletal systems for anything more than low-intensity exercise, you must first go through your basic training. If you take me on as your coach, then we can keep you from the statistics columns at the sportsmedicine clinics or from long lines at the podiatrist's office. First, you will learn to breathe properly. Then, you will stretch slowly and gently and brush the cobwebs off those unused muscles and tendons. Only afterward will you learn to walk the right way, using that untapped energy you have within you, wasted all these years. You will rediscover your strength, your vitality, your awareness. You will look forward to your workouts.

I have had so much success with average, overweight and under-exercised people that I felt the need to write a different kind of book on the essentials of racewalking, not only for the competitive athlete but for the completely noncompetitive man or woman as well. It can change your life. You can experience the joy of living as an athlete, even if only part-time, and only as far as you care to push it.

Some of the many books on the market today are informative and inspirational, but they only *tell* you how—they don't *show* you how. Here then is a book that actually shows you, step-by-step, *how* to warm up and *how* to walk. I will explain the correct technique of walking, allowing you to develop your own style according to your own individual body characteristics.

Study the book at home first, then take it to the park, or the track, or the street, and with a friend take a lesson from me—your coach. You will be amazed at how easy it is, how well you will do, and how well you'll feel!

HOWARD JACOBSON

"When my racewalking career began, Coach and teammate Howie Jacobson helped me make a quick and successful transition from running to walking. Many workouts and talks together taught me the fundamentals of good walking techniques and how to apply my knowledge of training to racewalking. Throughout the six years we worked and walked together, his inspiration, help and advice was significant in helping me reach my highest goal in athletics—the U.S. Olympic Team."

—STEVE HAYDEN,
'72 United States Olympic 50 km Team

ONE

The Whys
of Walking

EPA

1

BE AN ATHLETE
It's the Attitude That Counts

The Man said it: "Walking is man's best medicine." Hippocrates, the great Greek physician who lived from 460–390 B.C. has been called the Father of Medicine, and the famous Hippocratic oath concerning the ethics of being a physician is taken to this day by medical school graduates. Hippocrates' statement on walking is as true now as it was in ancient times—times when people went just about everywhere on foot. The influence of Greece is with us yet. Not only have we drawn much of our daily language and most of our literary forms but great contributions in art, architecture, biology, mathematics and medicine. The 5th and 4th centuries B.C. were the Golden Age of Greece. It took almost 2,000 years in the history of the world (during the Renaissance period) before the scholars of mankind were able to surpass the scientific triumphs which the Greek geniuses had achieved in little more than 200 years. The most fundamental article of the Greek creed was an intense belief in human life. He understood, as few have understood it, the art of living life. It was in Greece that the idea of political democracy came into being. The Olympic Games were begun with the idea of developing unity between the different city-states of the Greek Empire. The aim of the Greek city-state was the maximum development of the individual's power—physical and intellectual—for the good of the whole community. He would train his body to a high level of fitness so that he might serve his country in time of war. He would cultivate his intellect in order to play his full part in her culture. Greek unity: "a sound mind in a sound body."

The magnificent Greek sculpture of the Golden Age especially favored the figure of the victorious athlete, with his look of lean muscularity. The word athlete is Greek in origin and means "a person trained in exercises requiring physical strength, skill or speed." In Greek *kallos* means beauty and *sthenos* means strength. Hence calisthenics—still being taught today.

The Greeks admired the body beautiful. No people were more persistently addicted to the practice of physical exercise than the early Greeks. Men of every age and station went regularly to the gymnasium for daily recreation. Sport in our modern concept was not the main object of that recreation. Team games were rare, if not unknown. The Greeks strove for physical fitness and moral strength. All of the training was planned to develop endurance. The most famous of the warriors were those from the city of Sparta. They prized good health and bodily vigor above all else. What distinguished the Greeks from other people was chiefly their habitual self-restraint. The Spartans were a brave, stoical, frugal and highly disciplined people. The development of character and muscle was the outstanding feature of their arduous training. They played games which were rude tests of courage and strength. The Spartan grown to manhood was an incomparable warrior, inured to discipline and self-restraint. In training, he worked very hard, took sufficient rest, wore only a minimum of clothing, and was given a meager but nourishing diet. But he became outstandingly strong, fast, alert. The Spartiate girls were famous for their athletic prowess. The women possessed a stoical courage that strengthened the discipline of their men. The examples of the warriors and athletes were followed by Greek men in their gymnasiums and by the women at home and at the baths. They tried to develop sound minds and bodies. They lived longer and enjoyed healthier lives than other civilizations.

But where in today's world are those Spartan men and women—a host of lean and fit warriors and athletes? Sadly, they have gone the way of all flesh. And today, flesh is the problem. Too soft and too much of it. Today's "warriors" are fighting the battle of their own bulge. Most athletes are the armchair type, gorging themselves on junk food in front of their television sets. Too much weight. Too little exercise. You know it and I know it—else you wouldn't be reading and I wouldn't be writing this book.

When are you really going to unblock your mind to the fact that a lot of the statistics about heart disease, obesity, back pain, etc., are really about *you* now, or could be *you* in the future. Are you really grossly overweight and flabby, or have you just simply let yourself slip out of shape? Our problem (yours and mine), once you recognize yourself, is how you are going to motivate you, or how I am going to help you motivate yourself, to get off your duff and really do something. If you love yourself and love your family, you will.

During the past couple of years, you have been deluged with information about the physical condition of average Americans and what they should do to protect themselves from many of the ailments of modern times. The material has been everywhere—in books, magazines, newspapers, and on radio and television. I am not going to take your valuable time (you could be going out for a workout sooner) by going into all of that now. You probably have read or seen plenty of it already. But just in case you haven't read very much about the sad shape of our average American (or haven't bothered to—feeling that the information was not directed at you) and of the very real dangers of not exercising, I suggest that you turn now to chapter 2 on page 30. After reading it, come back to this page. If you are not convinced by then, pass this book on to someone else. But better still, since you enjoy sitting so much and are not going anywhere, read on. Something might shake you, wake you, or really interest you so that you *will* do something about you. It is never too late.

Now that we are all back together again, let's deal with this problem of motivation. Perhaps you haven't yet found the key to your own motivation. You can be urged to exercise by friends, family, doctors, scientists, whomever—all citing the benefits of and the dangers of not. Intellectually, you can understand and agree that you absolutely do need an exercise program. But when push comes to shove, you just don't manage to do anything about it. Right? Because it really has to do with *self-motivation*. You should have a really serious talk with yourself to find out exactly where you're at. Are you asking yourself the right questions and answering yourself honestly? Questions like:

An I happy with myself?
Do I have enough vitality?
Am I in good shape?
Am I pleased with the way I look?

Can I stand in front of the mirror—stark naked—and honestly decide I don't need to lose weight or firm up?

According to a survey released in May 1979 by the research firm of Yankelovich, Skelly and White for General Mills, Americans are more concerned with looking good and feeling good right now than they are about the avoidance of some dread disease in the future. People do realize, they say, that part of the blame for not practicing good health habits is their own lack of motivation, will power and information about good health practices.

Some women have said to me, "I want to join your program because I want to lose about 5 pounds." (But in actuality it looked more like 15 or 20.) If you don't want to admit that you have excess fat which can be trimmed, then you are either being dishonest with yourself, or you just want to hide behind your fat and not do anything about it at all. To most people, fat is really a turnoff. They really admire the slim and lean figure—the figure of the athletic man, the figure of the athletic woman. This goes for people of all ages. You can start training at any age and see results. Start training and you can look your best for your age. A gentleman I know living in Florida had a coronary bypass operation about 5 years ago at the age of 70. He went to The Longevity Center in California run by Nathan Pritikin, whose program I'll tell you more about later. My friend lost 40 pounds through diet and exercise and looks at least 10 years younger. If he and so many others can do it, why can't you?

Those people who have embarked on exercise programs are saying things like:

"I feel like a new person."

"I'm slimmer."

"I feel sexier."

"I sleep better."

"I really feel good."

"I find myself eating less."

"I look forward to my training."

"I'm much more relaxed."

"I don't get so upset anymore."

"I know I look good."

"I am really proud of me."

Let's analyze those statements. As a result of all the physical training these people have gone through, they have commented about "head stuff." "I feel good." "I am proud of me." Their attitudes regarding "self" have changed. As their bodies have changed, so have their minds. Sound bodies, sound minds. The Greek ideal. The Greek athlete.

That's right! I want you *all* to become athletes. Whatever your age, whatever your present physical condition, if you plan on starting an exercise program, you can do it with me—as an athlete. Please understand that *everyone* can be an athlete. Remember the definition of an athlete: "a person trained in exercises requiring physical strength, skill or speed." To be an athlete does not mean to be a competitor. I don't wish to make competitors out of you. If you never compete in a race and just adopt my training program three, four, or five times a week for an hour at a time, that will be just fine with me—and better for you. One of my protégés, Mrs. C. Henn, became an "athlete" at age 60. She is a housewife who is now an athlete in training for an hour a day.

In our country, except for professional athletes, we engage in athletics on a part-time basis. High school and college athletes go to school full-time and practice their sport as an extracurricular activity. Later they continue the same way. Frank Shorter is a lawyer-business man-marathon runner. Marty Liquori is a world-class runner who owns the franchise to the Athletic Attic stores and also is a television commentator. Larry Young, Olympic medalist, is a full-time sculptor and part-time racewalker. Susan Liers is a full-time college student and part-time racewalker. Professor Audrey Haschemeyer is a full-time biochemist and a part-time racewalker.

You can be a full-time athlete in your head and only a part-time athlete in your training. The time when you actually are an athlete will spill over and affect the way you conduct the rest of your time. For example, you pass up that extra helping of potatoes because you *don't want* to undo all the good you've been doing your body by training. Or you will go to sleep earlier because you *want* to get up early the next morning to train. I know that most of you have family, business, social and/or other interests to keep you busy, but if you

PROFILE OF AN ATHLETE
Eugenia Henn

Mrs. Carl (Eugenia) Henn of New Brunswick, New Jersey, shows excellent racewalking technique while training in the park near her home. Eugenia, age 61, started training with me in October 1978 after problems with her knee and hip. After a slow and easy stretching session, she goes out for her workout. Mrs. Henn racewalks daily and now covers 3–4 miles during each workout.

are truly interested in starting a training program and staying with it, try my approach to self-motivation.

For years I arose early, worked out and caught the commuter train at 7:15 A.M. for my work in New York City. I worked a full day, caught the 6:04 P.M. back home to my wife and four children, and still had time for my family and a busy social life. When I had special events coming up, I trained twice a day. Weekends were devoted to early Long Island Athletic Club team practices, where I coached and trained with my men. But I was home by 11 or 12 o'clock for the family brunches, followed by mowing the lawn, playing football with my boys, practicing crafts with the girls, barbecues with the family, and a quick nap before dinner and/or visiting with wife and friends. I had time for many things because I *made* the time. I *wanted* to badly enough. I've been through it all these past 35 years—always an athlete. Try the athlete's approach. Try my approach. Athletes are a special breed. People have much to learn from them. It is the *attitude* of the athlete that I hope to have you understand.

As the ancient Greeks revered their athletes, so do we tend to glorify special ones. In high school and college the athletes earn varsity letters—symbols of achievement. They wear their lettered sweaters or team jackets with honor and pride. All-star teams, most valuable player awards, the Heisman Trophy (football), the Sullivan Award (the amateur athlete of the year), and the various Halls of Fame are some of the ways that the athlete is singled out and honored for his or her special achievement. But you see, *all* athletes, not just the fastest or the ones with the highest scores, win something. And if you opt for the life of an athlete you too can win. Athletes have a sense of self—an ability to direct their energies toward their goals. Studies have shown that athletes rank internal rewards far greater than mere trophies. There is the winning of self-esteem. Trim and good-looking, most athletes are obvious by the way they move—fluidly, almost catlike. All the world loves a winner. You can look and feel like a winner!

Pélé, O. J. Simpson, Billie Jean King, Jesse Owens, Bill Russell, Joe DiMaggio, Gale Sayers, Dorothy Hamill, Arthur Ashe, Nancy Lopez, Frank Shorter, Bill Rodgers—the list is endless—all are special. What makes them so special? What do they and millions of other athletes have in common? Aside from being born with certain physical attributes or having had better opportunities or coaching, most athletes the world over have:

- Desire
- Dedication
- Discipline
- Determination
- Courage
- The willingness to work hard
- The willingness to sacrifice
- The ability to accept pain

These are attitudes, winning attitudes. And those attitudes make them special. But you too are special, aren't you! To yourself. To your family. To your friends. You are special to me. I want to share with you what has gone through me and the hundreds of athletes—both champions and also-rans—whom I have known and competed with these many years. You can learn much from them.

All of the previous names, which I am sure you have easily recognized, were or are outstanding competitive athletes, and if you noticed, all but the runners in spectator sports. Don't be scared off, feeling that you will have to measure up to them. I repeat, you don't have to compete with them. Nor with anyone else for that matter. You can do your own thing. The reason I chose those names was to point up the fact that they were highly visible athletes recognized by most people with an interest in spectator sports.

The big-time spectator sports such as basketball, baseball, and football—especially at the collegiate and professional levels, paradoxically are contributing greatly to the poor health of the population of this country. We are a nation of spectators, not participants. But that wasn't so in the days of ancient Greece. Throngs attended the various festivals and athletic games, but they also involved themselves daily for their own physical well-being. Today, sports are a TV obsession. Pick up any week's schedule and see the constant goings on. Besides, most women are not as interested in the events as men, and they end up resenting much of the time that the men ignore them while watching a football or baseball game. Why can't men and women find some more things that they can enjoy together, such as exercise? Certainly you may want to watch some events, but if you become a perpetual spectator, you're simply neglecting yourself and your loved ones. If you believe as I do in the Greek philosophy of a sound body and a sound mind, then believe that you can add much more balance to your life by participating.

Taking part is where it's at—not just sitting idly by. The motto of the founder of the modern Olympic Games, Baron Pierre De Coubertin, was: "The important thing is to participate—not to win." In a good physical fitness program, everyone who participates will win. You will all be athletes in training: training for the big event—your own fitness. All you have to do to be an athlete is to cultivate the right attitude and move your body—train. Why not adopt some of those inspiring and outstanding qualities of the athlete's attitude toward training and self? Imagine the pleasure of a job well done. The pride in saying "I did it! I feel good. I know I look good."

Every morning in all kinds of weather, I pass scores of men and women walking and jogging along the promenade of Carl Schurz Park on the East River Drive. Some of them are my protégés, who started on my programs 3 years ago. The others are nodding acquaintances —exchanging greetings in the early morning. When many of them started, they were hardly able to walk half a mile without breathing hard. They have made wonderful progress, now covering 2 to 6 miles each morning in heat or cold, rain or shine. Some of them are even "snow birds." I know that I have been instrumental in changing their lives—as they keep reminding me. They are all dedicated athletes. And most of them never race! They are all beautiful! I am as proud of them as they are of themselves.

Do you really have the desire? Do you really *want* to be physically fit, with all the accompanying benefits—physical and mental? If you really want it badly enough, you can develop the athlete's winning attitudes. If you have the desire, you can muster up the dedication, the discipline and the willingness to work hard. You *can* do it! As Goethe said: "Whatever you can do, or dream you can—begin it. Boldness has genius, power and magic in it." Be an athlete!

2

WALK, DON'T RUN
Racewalking Will Do It All—
and More Safely

Jog, jog, jog. Run, run, run. That's all people are talking about today. Jogging is an "in" sport. Doctors recommend it, newspapers and television tout its benefits. "Run for your lives," says *Newsweek* magazine. Regardless of the speeds involved, jogging and running are really synonymous, and to avoid confusion I will refer to them both only as running.

The following is a typical story of the average person influenced by well-meaning friends and family. Barbara P. is 30 years old, single, and lives alone. She works for an advertising agency and has always been a bit overweight. Barbara was a cheerleader in high school, but aside from enjoying disco dancing she has never done any physical exercise since. She and her friends have just decided to rent a summer house at the beach. She has decided for the 10th year in a row to really lose weight in the few intervening months and look great in her new bikini. Her friends have advised her to get into shape by running. After all, isn't that what everyone is doing? Yesterday, along with a trim-looking warm-up outfit, she bought a beautiful and expensive pair of royal blue running shoes.

Setting the alarm, she goes off to sleep dreaming of the slender new person she is going to become. The next morning she charges out the door into the sunlight, full of determination and energy. Her plan is to run three times around the block. So up on her toes and with knees high, she begins her sprint around the corner. Disaster! Rigor mortis sets in after about a block and a half! Out of breath and simply exhausted, Barbara can hardly walk home. What happened? Very simply, she overdid it. Most people have a tendency to do too much too soon. They end up overly fatigued, muscle sore, possibly with an injury or, at the very worst, with a heart attack. Barbara tried running a few more times and gave it up—discouraged and still out of shape.

If you were to go to any park or track or area where people run, you would see pained expressions and gasping mouths fighting for breath. You wonder if these people are enjoying their workout or if running is just viewed as a means to an end. This country is currently "enjoying" a running boom, with some 20–25 million people out on the roads. But how much enjoyment is there actually? The slowest jog for some people is really hard work. Running has given many people cardiovascular fitness and trimmer bodies, but many others are suffering from stress or injuries up the kinetic chain from foot to lower back. Some of the most common runners injuries are: Achilles tendinitis, shin splints, chondromalacia patellae (runners knee), sciatica and low backache. According to Dr. George A. Sheehan, a foremost authority on running, "A runner averaging 50 miles a week has a 73 percent chance of suffering from an injury that will sideline him for a considerable length of time." The sportsmedicine clinics are

extremely busy, and the waiting time to see a podiatrist is often 2 to 3 months. Runners are being injured at an alarming rate. What for? Why all this unnecessary pain? Who is to blame?

First, I blame the authors of the running books and magazines, well-meaning as they are, for overglamorizing the sport of running by grossly exaggerating the so-called spiritual benefits: "state of altered awareness" or "runner's high." In this age of pot, coke and pills, lots of people keep looking for more thrills and experiences. They will push their bodies to achieve these experiences, only to find out that their bodies are not ready to handle the additional mileage or increased speed, and they end up being injured. The problem is that the often extravagant and indiscriminate claims made by these "gurus" or exercise crusaders cause many of the normally intense and competitive individuals to develop a sense of urgency and competitiveness about training and racing. They do *too much too soon*. Most of the people who read these books and magazines have been on a "time out" from physical activity for a number of years, and their musculoskeletal units are not ready for the wear and tear of running. I blame certain authors for not having enough experience with people to realize that it takes a longer time to get into shape than they or their readers realize. I blame them also for encouraging people into competitive races, rather than just for fitness. At last year's Bloomingdale's 10 kilometer run in Central Park, there were many runners who had not done any training at all before the race. They wanted to "experience" the race, to wear the T-shirt. No wonder the dropout rate, according to Fred Lebow, President of the New York Road Runners Club, was exceedingly high. Not enough preparation.

On our highways there are often signs posted: Speed kills. Applying that statement to physical fitness and running in particular, I believe that there is too much emphasis on speed—and racing. Invariably, when two runners meet, the conversation goes something like this:

"Did you run in that 6-mile race?"

"Yes, I did."

"What was your time?"

"Well—er—I did 48.35. But I really can do better. I just have to increase my mileage and do some speed work."

Then comes the pressure. Pushing to do more when you are not necessarily ready to handle that kind of work. It has been proven that the injury rates for high-intensity exercises are much greater than for low-intensity exercises. For cardiovascular fitness—long, slow distance training is much better than short-interval, fast speed training. So why not go more slowly and enjoy it more, without the self-imposed pressures that racing fosters?

Equally to blame for so many running injuries is the fitness-hungry public itself. The runner sees himself or herself as a more dashing person—a sport. But there is a tinge of snobbery there. When asked the question, "Do you jog?" many times he answers, "No, *I* run." (And then he tries harder and harder to become the image he's trying to create.) Running can become addictive and there is really nothing wrong with that. The exercise indeed can provide fitness, weight loss, a relaxed attitude—fine. These lead to good feelings about oneself. But when people push themselves too hard with hopes of heightening those feelings without realizing that their bodies are not ready to accept all that work, that is overkill. Many people are naturally competitive, and that urge may be raised to an irrational level when involved in training for or competing in a race.

Talk about irrationality. Why does everyone *have* to run a marathon? "I want to go through the experience," they say. "I want to prove to myself that I can do it," is heard from others. Most of them have no idea in the world what making that commitment involves. Besides the injuries that Dr. Sheehan talks about, there are many, many injuries experienced during the race itself.

Dr. Richard Schwartz, a cardiologist and consultant in physical fitness at the University of Maryland, states: "Once you get beyond 4 or 5 miles you're talking about an ego trip rather than physical fitness. Now, many people are competing with themselves over how many miles they can run and often comparing their performances with their associates."

Many beginners give up running in the first 3 to 6 weeks: too sore, too boring, too tiring, too hard. For whatever the reason, they have given up a program that they had sought out because they wanted to improve their fitness level. They didn't enjoy it. They probably overdid it.

Television, the newspapers and the magazines have been full of articles and programs telling us how good running is for us. Surely, running must be the 20th century equivalent of Ponce de Leon's Fountain of Youth. The number one exercise that all of the media promote is running.

Well, they are all wrong!

- Many people are not able to run.
- Many people are not ready to run.
- Many people don't know how to run.
- Many people don't like to run.
- Many people don't want to run.
- Many people should not run.

It is my firm belief that the time has come for a more moderate approach toward physical exercise, especially with endurance training. The gross exaggerations, philosophies and spiritualizing about running should be stopped, and it should be treated with a more down-to-earth sense of perspective. We are wallowing in words. Let's call a halt! We—as coaches, doctors and authors—should help people maintain a sense of proportion in their sports and physical activities. We should urge them to exercise more cautiously and not to overdo it.

There are only about a dozen true racewalking coaches in this entire country. Add to that only a couple of thousand participants, and you have the bare beginnings of what should be the greatest participant sport in the country—Racewalking! As of January 1978, the United States Census estimated the population to be 220 million and everyone walks. But most people don't walk the most beneficial way and not nearly enough. Walking is taken so much for granted as locomotion that it is overlooked as the perfect exercise.

Perhaps I really shouldn't be too hard on the running authors, the running doctors, the track coaches and the various news media for not writing about and not helping to build the sport and exercise of racewalking. They don't understand it well enough. Here is a case in point. Tom Osler, a great distance and ultra-distance runner and author, wrote in the May 1978 *Runners World* magazine: "I must emphasize that I am not recommending racewalking (which isn't really walking at all, but is stiff-legged running). Rather, I am suggesting ordinary brisk walking at about 3 to 4 miles per hour." If Professor Osler had done his homework, he would have discovered that racewalking is indeed biomechanically nothing more than fast ordinary walking.

Dr. Gabe Mirkin, author of *The Sportsmedicine Book* and himself a runner, says: "Walking doesn't train your heart as a rule. If you're in such bad shape that walking brings your heart rate up to 120 beats per minute, then it will help. But as you become fit, walking will not train your heart unless you do it very vigorously." If he's talking about strolling he's right, but didn't he ever hear of racewalking for fitness?

Many of the people dispensing exercise prescriptions say, "Walk, then jog until mildly uncomfortable, then recover by walking, then continue jogging." Baloney! It's better to racewalk all the way. You don't *have* to be uncomfortable at all.

Lt. General R. L. Bohannon, M.D., President and Founder of the National Jogging Association wrote on motivation: "Go out to walk, rather than jog. It's easier to 'go out for a walk' than it is to 'go out for a jog.' It's easier on the psyche to set out to merely walk—and then intersperse jogging as you feel the urge. Before you know it, you'll be wanting to jog more than walk." His advice is pretty good. But it is easier and even better to racewalk all the way.

A century ago an editorial in *Scientific American* accused long distance walkers of "pleading the old cant of promotion of health and all the rest of it," and warned that this activity would not be beneficial. Very few people in this country have ever understood racewalking. For the last 40 or 50 years it has been a stepchild sport. However, in the 1968 Olympic Games in Mexico City, our Larry Young placed 3rd in the 50 kilometer racewalk and our Rudy Haluza 4th in the 20 kilometer racewalk. Those U.S. Team racewalkers earned great respect from the distance runners and marathoners of this country, who woke up to what kind of athletes the racewalkers are.

There are also a few doctors and podiatrists who don't have blinders on and appreciate the values of walking for sport and exercise. Dr. Sheehan states in his book *Dr. Sheehan on Running,* perhaps even prophetically, "Racewalkers are part of a ground swell that may become the wave of the future. Racewalkers are virtually injury free." Among racewalkers, distance runners and sprinters, racewalkers have the best overall leg development and the lowest rate of injury. It has been found that when one muscle group is excessively stronger than its opposing muscle group, the chances of injury in the weaker group are substantially increased. Sprinters develop very strong quadriceps (the front thigh muscles) and relatively weak hamstrings (the rear thigh muscles), greatly increasing their chances for hamstring pulls. Distance runners develop stronger and shorter hamstrings and are susceptible to groin and quadriceps injuries. Racewalking technique makes great use of the quadriceps and of the hamstrings, strengthening both the fronts and the backs of the legs.

National Blue Cross Assoc.

America's best performance in Olympic 20 km, Mexico, 1968: Rudy Haluza, 4th place.
Eli Attar

Harry S Truman

Dr. Grant Gwinup of the University of California calls walking "the one exercise that does everything."

Dr. Michael Pollock, Director of Cardiac Rehabilitation at the University of Wisconsin–Mount Sinai Medical Center in Milwaukee says, "Walking is considered the safest and most natural of exercises."

Blue Cross and Blue Shield Plans advocate brisk walking. They advertise the program that our late President Harry Truman had to lower health care costs: "All his life, Mr. Truman firmly believed in taking brisk walks. Every day, no matter what, he marched along at the old infantry pace of 120 strides per minute. He felt the exercise and stimulation would keep him in better shape and therefore better health." He did live in good physical trim until age 88.

The following are comments on racewalking by Dr. Thomas De Lauro, Professor, New York College of Podiatric Medicine:

> When studying racewalking, one is immediately impressed with the racewalkers' concern for technique. The perfection of technique means improved efficiency and therefore greater endurance with reduction of injuries as a by-product. Proper racewalking technique limits abnormal pronation by concentrating on foot placement, the transference of body weight, and push-off directly through the big toe. If abnormal or excessive pronation is limited, then plantar fascia can't be stretched, metatarsal bones cannot be overly strained and fractured, the ankle can be set more consciously thereby avoiding sprain and the leg will not twist inwardly to create chondromalacia patellae (inflammation of the knee).

An article in *The New York Times,* April 23, 1978, said: "Foot doctors tend to give regular brisk walking higher marks than even running or jogging for achieving and maintaining fitness." It seems that some doctors have caught on to the most obvious exercise of all —walking. Now the wave is really beginning to form.

Let's take time out right here to explain the difference between the word *walking* and the word *racewalking*. Biomechanically, both are walking, but racewalking utilizes the arms in a more dynamic manner than walking, brisk walking or, surprisingly, even jogging and long distance running. So it's not that I want you people to *race*; I want you to utilize your *arms* as well as your legs, develop the *style* of a racewalker.

Early in 1977, when I began my fitness consulting business, I was the only person in the country to develop a program advocating racewalking for fitness. Racewalking is the foundation of my program because proper walking is the foundation for good health and fitness. Too many people are experiencing running injuries, but during all of my 20-odd years of experience as a competitive racewalker, I have seen very few injuries in the racewalking community. As a result of my studies in physiology and kinesiology, together with consultations with various orthopedists and podiatrists, I've learned that what is required for relatively injury-free performance is proper alignment of the bones of the foot, leg and hip, allowing minimal wear and tear on their respective muscle-tendon units. Proper racewalking can provide that alignment, but because of the variables involved in gait, running often doesn't provide it.

Two of the authors of best-selling books on running make these bold claims. "Running is the simplest," says one. "Running is the easiest," says the other. *They are both wrong!* Not fully understanding it, they chose not to mention racewalking. Walking, brisk walking and racewalking are the simplest, easiest and best exercises.

So here we are approximately 2,400 years later, back to Hippocrates, "Walking is man's best medicine." I maintain that his prescription for health can work. Up to now, too many prescriptions have been dispensed for drugs to cure diseases rather than for exercise to prevent them. Knowledgeable sources feel that the next major breakthrough in medicine will come through changes in our lifestyle, not through anything doctors or drugs can do for us. The one factor that could have the greatest impact on increasing the number of Americans who will exercise is a doctor's recommendation. But not enough doctors are advocating vigorous exercise for enough of their patients, probably because they themselves are poor examples—smoking too much, eating and drinking too much, and exercising too little. So we must look to ourselves. If we can become healthy and fit, then we will need neither the doctors nor the drugs. And if you like to do things yourself, here's a sensible project: Give yourself a prescription for preventive medicine—good nutrition, sufficient rest and vigorous exercise. Be an athlete. Be a racewalker. Racewalking is the preventive medicine that we have been looking for.

- Racewalking will make you feel good.
- Racewalking will make you look good.

That's it! For some people, that is all they really need to know. But if you want more, then there is more:

- Racewalking may help prevent heart disease.
- Racewalking will help to improve fitness and stamina.
- Racewalking will help you lose pounds and inches.
- Racewalking will help strengthen your muscles and tissues.
- Racewalking will help to release tension and anxieties.
- Racewalking will help develop more efficient blood circulation.
- Racewalking will help your body to use oxygen more effectively.
- Racewalking will help you to handle stress better.
- Racewalking will help you to enjoy and perform better sexually.
- Racewalking will help keep you alert and vital.
- Racewalking will help strengthen your bones.
- Racewalking will help give a woman a firmer and higher bustline.
- Racewalking will help strengthen your skin.
- Racewalking will help you to improve your posture.
- Racewalking will help give you feelings of self-assurance.
- Racewalking will virtually eliminate stress and overuse injuries.

You have been walking all of your life and have probably never realized what tremendous potential you have within your body. Walking, as much or as little as you have been doing it, has directly affected your current fitness level. Take notice, I said *current* fitness level. Fitness fades very rapidly, requiring constant effort. In a few weeks without training, you lose much of your previous conditioning. If you were to become bedridden, your muscles would atrophy, your blood vessels would shrink, and your blood circulation would diminish to a dangerous level. Your bodily functions would be impaired and you might even require hospital care. Why do you think they put postoperative patients on their feet so quickly these days and walk them around? Doctors have learned the circulatory value of even that mild bit of exercise.

The human body is the one machine that breaks down when it is *not* used. It is the one machine that works better the *more* it is used. Our bodies are built poorly for sitting and not much better for standing. Our bodies are built for *walking*. The most skillfully designed piece of machinery cannot match the human machine in perfection of detail or in potential smoothness of function. Practically all the muscles in your body are used for walking. It is the most natural, the easiest and the most efficient exercise that man does, and most people overlook it as a form of exercise.

The racewalker has elevated normal walking to a sport, an Olympic event. In endeavoring to walk faster and faster, the racewalker has added yet another dimension to normal walking. In normal walking the arms usually hang loosely at the sides, naturally and rhythmically swinging—synchronized with each opposite leg. The racewalker strives to take more steps per minute and a long pendulum (fully straightened arm) would slow him down. He shortens the pendulum by bending his arm at the elbow to a 90-degree angle. The shorter the pendulum, the faster you can move it. Now the racewalker is able to move his arms in a more dynamic manner, using them to help thrust himself forward. This powerful usage of the arms also aids in maintaining balance and forward fluidity. Additionally, the powerful and dynamic usage of the arms requires more energy and consequently burns more calories than does walking or distance running. The racewalker uses his arms like a sprinter—smoothly and powerfully. The energy expended by the racewalker shows the current charts grading various exercises according to caloric consumption to be completely obsolete.

Before we begin to examine the various benefits of racewalking, it is important to understand the human being's remarkable ability to adapt. There are two kinds of endurance—physical and mental. The Greeks strove for it, why can't we? When you can survive being knocked around, mistreated and abused, that's endurance. Some liken endurance to being tough. I agree. I think that we should be more like those Spartan warriors. We should toughen up, both physically and mentally.

All of our bodily systems are subject to adaptation. That is, a change in structure or function can produce better adjustment to our environment. For example, our bodies have a remarkable ability to adapt to physical stress. Physical training places a certain amount of stress on the body, and the body accepts it, adapts to it, and then is able to take on an even greater work load. Racewalking is the ideal physical exercise because you can begin at a relatively slow pace, sensibly ease into a regimen of training, and immediately achieve benefits.

Here are the benefits obtainable from man's best medicine:

Racewalking may help prevent heart disease by causing the heart to pump more blood through the circulatory system, making the heart more efficient and stronger. The blood vessels become more elastic and flexible. Fatty deposits will be reduced, lessening the possibility of heart disease. Even if a heart attack should occur, the stronger heart is more often able to withstand the attack.

Racewalking will help to improve fitness and stamina by placing moderate amounts of stress on the entire cardiovascular system. The system will adapt to it and be able to take on more.

Racewalking will help you lose pounds and inches. You will lose weight from all over your body. Whenever you use a muscle or a group of muscles, they send out signals to every fat cell in your body. These cells release fat molecules into the bloodstream, traveling to the working muscles to be used as energy fuel. Sustained muscle work seems to be based primarily on fat utilization. Therefore, if you really want to lose weight, combine your racewalking with a diet containing fewer calories. The more you walk the more you'll lose.

Racewalking will help strengthen your muscles and tissues. Because of the dynamic action of the racewalking stride, a greater balance is achieved for the musculature of the leg. The buttocks muscle, because of the pulling action of the leg at foot plant, is one of the first to become firm and strong. The front of the thighs and the shins become quite strong and firm from the pulling stage of the racewalking style. The propulsive phase of the style adds great strength to the muscles on the back of the leg. A racewalker's upper body develops strength and endurance because of the dynamic action of the arms. There is an allover development of adaptive increases in muscle mass and muscle strength. This means long and lean muscles built for endurance. For the female it can mean lean proportions, attractive to any man and the envy of most women. For the male it can mean a look of lean athleticism, equally as attractive.

Racewalking will help to release tension and anxieties. Walking has been medically recognized as a means of coping with low-grade depression. As with most endurance training, it is the increased circulation to the brain of life-giving oxygen and other chemicals that lifts your spirits. A hormone called epinephrine—a chemical associated with happiness—is produced after 10–15 minutes of training, resulting in pleasurable feelings. Racewalking can burn up the excess energy that many of you have and really mellow you out. There is nothing so relaxing as a nice warm shower after feeling pleasantly tired from a workout.

> "Tonight, I'm going to walk for about four hours and look at the moon. I don't know where—just walk, walk, walk. I've got to unwind."
>
> —Rafer Johnson,
> 1960 Olympic Champion, Decathlon

While doing some hot weather training for the Maccabean Games in Israel in 1969, I was doing a fast 10 miles along the service road to the Long Island Expressway. At about 6 miles out, I got the strangest feeling. I felt like my head was detached from my body, like I was an "observer of me." I was very loose, very relaxed, moving very fast, but it seemed effortless. I was so exhilarated that I burst out laughing and felt light-headed. Every once in a while since then, I go through it again. Always when I am alone. Always when I am fast and fluid. Who said walkers don't get high?

Racewalking will help give a woman a firmer and higher bustline. Because of the dynamic usage of the arms, the pectoral muscles that help to support the breasts become stronger, and as they do so, the breasts become firmer and higher.

Racewalking will help develop more efficient blood circulation. As stated earlier, with exercise the heart muscle pumps more blood throughout the system. The more you exercise, the greater the circulatory effect. The blood, carrying oxygen and all of the nutrients, travels to the minutest of cells by way of the minutest of capillaries. Literally your whole body is being "cleansed" and nourished with blood.

Racewalking will help your body to use oxygen more effectively. Each cell in your body needs oxygen to survive. Racewalking will help you to breathe deeply, regularly and rhythmically, giving you a greater intake of oxygen and a greater expulsion of waste gases. The oxygen literally "feeds" the body.

Racewalking will help you to handle stress better. The exercise that you get from racewalking will enable your body to develop and maintain a vital reserve which has a protective effect during stress. The vital reserve can be likened to shock absorbers on a car or a bulletproof vest. During stressful times you are better protected from the possibility of a heart attack.

Racewalking will help you to enjoy and perform better sexually. Your body is slim and alive. Your muscles are firm and strong. Your mental acuity keeps you in touch with all of your senses. You have the stamina and drive of youth. Try your luck with a racewalker. Or be a racewalker and you'll find out.

Racewalking will help keep you alert and vital. All that increased flow of blood and oxygen cleanses the brain, as well as the rest of the body, and tones the mind. Perception is heightened. You feel alive, alert. You develop a greater capacity for work and don't tire toward the end of the day. It instills feelings of well-being and enhances creativity.

Racewalking will help strengthen your bones. Healthful stress, in the form of an exercise such as racewalking, sends an electrochemical charge through your bones causing them to rebuild themselves, increasing bone density. Bones at rest will lose about 50 percent of their calcium, recovering when activity resumes.

Racewalking will help strengthen your skin. The exercise will make your skin thicker, stronger and more elastic. Skin responds to regular exercise in the same way that your tendons and ligaments do.

Racewalking will help you to improve your posture. It all begins at your center—your abdomen. With racewalking, you will strengthen your abdominal muscles and walk with head and back erect, buttocks tucked in slightly. You will learn to walk tall, giving yourself a higher center of gravity, allowing for a longer stride. The movement of the arms, almost isolated from the body, will help toward an erect carriage.

Racewalking will help give you feelings of self-assurance. When you see the progress that you have made, the benefits you've achieved, and the good feelings you've experienced, you simply have to be self-assured. A New York Academy of Sciences conference portrayed endurance athletes to be more independent and emotionally stable and less anxiety prone than their nonathletic counterparts.

Racewalking will virtually eliminate stress and overuse injuries. Most stress and overuse injuries in athletics occur from improper joint alignment while running. Each joint moves on a specific axis. Any abnormal motion or change in the axis, even minimal, will make the joint and other parts of the foot or leg more prone to injury. Racewalking better controls joint alignment, thereby reducing the possibility of injury. Running also causes a shock/impact factor, with each step, of 3½ to 4 times a person's body weight, whereas racewalking involves a transfer of weight to only 1½ times body weight. Consider the stresses imposed in the course of taking 3,500 steps per half hour.

You have probably led a pretty sedentary life since graduating from high school or college. It is important to realize that you most likely have a low level of cardiovascular fitness (becoming breathless with even a mild bit of exercise) and a musculoskeletal system that is weak, without tone or elasticity. Years of inactivity have resulted in the contraction and shortening of your leg muscles and tendons. This is especially true of women because they wear high heels so often. The older people are, the less elastic their muscles, tendons and ligaments. Lazy muscles must be reeducated; tendons and ligaments not used to any degree of stress must be strengthened.

Get yourself into shape slowly, without pushing yourself. Dr. Harry F. Hlavac, founder of the Sports Medicine Clinic at the California College of Podiatric Medicine in San Francisco cautions, "A good rule of foot is to allow one month of conditioning for each year of previous inactivity, to avoid foot and other bone damage." Racewalking at slow speeds will gradually strengthen the cardiovascular and musculoskeletal systems, avoiding the overuse injuries which occur when distance or stress is put on the body too soon.

Steven Subotnick, the running Doctor of Podiatric Medicine for Hayward, California, agrees that a big factor in overuse injuries is improper conditioning. Dr. Subotnick also states that a cause for injuries to runners might be the sport itself. Running increases the angular deformity of the lower extremities because one foot will contact the ground just about on a straight line with the other foot, that straight line being at about the center of the body. In walking, the feet are more parallel to each other in a wider base of gait. This is more like walking straddling a 1- to 2-inch stripe, reducing the angular stresses.

Dr. Richard O. Schuster, practicing podiatrist and Professor at the New York College of Podiatric Medicine states that knee pain is often affected by the person's upper body weight, the shape of his legs, and whether or not the foot comes down in a perpendicular manner with each step. I maintain that this person would not have those knee pains if he or she would racewalk. The alignment would be better.

Employing the racewalking technique will involve almost all the muscles of your body, as compared to running which concentrates mostly on the legs. Racewalkers develop more strength in the upper torso and the arms because of the much more vigorous arm action. Most runners have overdeveloped accelerator muscles (located in the back of the leg and thigh, providing propulsion) and relatively weak decelerator muscles (located in the front of the leg and thigh, providing balance and opposing forward motion). This condition often results in overuse syndromes, shin splints and Achilles tendinitis.

Racewalkers develop more well-balanced leg muscles because they utilize the muscles of both the fronts and backs of the legs.

It is quite well known that most women gain their excess weight between their waist and their knees, as well as on the backs of the upper arms. Racewalking is an exceptionally dynamic way to trim off the excess fat from the thighs, buttocks, hips and from the backs of the upper arms. The work physiology of the racewalking technique is especially firming to those areas.

Compliance is an important factor in a training regimen. People participate in programs they enjoy. And that enjoyment is directly related to the intensity of the training.

The most important factor for fitness development is the total amount of work (energy cost) accomplished in a training program. That program consists of an interrelation of duration, frequency and intensity of the exercise. Intensity and energy expenditure are synonymous. The energy cost of running is generally higher than that of walking. Since the intensity of walking is less than running, you could get training effects similar to running if the duration and frequency of the walking are increased. Several years ago, a 20-week study of men 40–57 years old who walked briskly for 40 minutes 4 days a week was conducted. Their improvement in this program was equal to that of 30-minute, 3 days per week, moderate intensity jogging programs with men about the same age. The lower intensity of the walking program (65 percent to 75 percent of maximum) was offset by the increased duration and frequency of training. This showed the energy cost of the walking program to be equal to that of the jogging program.

Since improvement in cardiovascular-respiratory fitness is directly related to duration of training, a suitable program employing low-intensity racewalking, especially for the beginner, is recommended. Through racewalking, with its particular attention to style and the increased usage of the upper torso and arms, you will learn to orchestrate your body in a rhythmical and flowing manner at a pace which allows for more oxygen intake and heightened awareness of yourself and everything around you. In addition, the musculoskeletal system can withstand low-intensity work better than high-intensity work. Fewer injuries occur as a result of working at a slower pace. For many persons, including senior citizens, those who are overweight, and those with respiratory and other health problems, racewalking is often a safer and more reasonable exercise.

PROFILE OF A CHAMPION
Henry Laskau

The Dean of American racewalkers, Henry Laskau was born October 12, 1916, in Berlin, Germany, where he was a 5 and 10 km runner. He emigrated to America and served in the United States Army during World War II, after which he resumed his running career. But not for long. In 1945 he began racewalking and quickly rose to the top. Winning 43 national championships over a span of more than 20 years, Henry was a member of the United States Olympic teams in 1948, 1952 and 1956. He held the world's indoor 1-mile mark of 6:19 and electrified the crowds at Madison Square Garden when he would lap walker after walker. At one time or another, he held all the American records for 1 mile to 20 kilometers (12.4 miles).

Besides converting me from a runner to a racewalker, Henry has been responsible for converting and encouraging many more racewalkers now residing all over this country, who are also "spreading the gospel" of racewalking.

Although now retired from active competition, Henry and his beautiful wife, Hilde, have been tirelessly and unselfishly organizing and judging racewalks. He is President of the Walkers Club of America, the express purpose of which is to encourage racewalking not only for competition but for fitness as well.

Shown are the enthusiastic crowds applauding "number one," Henry Laskau, as he approaches the finish line in another great boardwalk performance.

Finally, racewalking for fitness can be at a pace that you can really enjoy. You can walk anywhere in the world, striding out, swinging your arms, breathing deeply, toning your body and mind at the same time.

Feel the thrust of power from racewalking—feel your own power!

Be a racewalker!

In this chapter, you were told about many of the look-good, feel-good benefits of racewalking and why it is the easiest and safest of exercises. In this "me generation," pleasure-seeking age, people are sometimes more concerned with how they look, especially to others, and how they feel than with what is going on *inside* their bodies. No less important than the look-good, feel-good benefits are racewalking's effect on the one muscle in our body that we rarely give enough time to, except during "affairs of the heart." The next chapter will point up what has happened to the "heartland" of America and what we can do about it.

3

MOVE!
Put Your Heart into It!

Whether you realize it or not, since the beginning of the 20th century, we have been in the grip of a growing worldwide epidemic—a tremendous increase in cardiovascular disease. Coincidentally, there has also been an explosive increase in the per capita usage of the automobile, popularized by Henry Ford in 1908. Is there a connection? Perhaps. Almost half the deaths of men and an increasing proportion of women in the Western world are caused by diseased hearts and blood vessels. According to the American Heart Association, each year approximately 670,000 people die of heart attacks in this country. About 29 million Americans of all ages suffer from some form of heart or blood vessel ailment. Men aged 30–59 have a fatal heart attack rate more than four times that of women in the same age bracket, but from age 60 on, the rate of heart attack deaths among women begins to approach that of men. Many thousands of these deaths occur among people in their most productive years, men and women with responsible careers, with children still in school, and with mortgage payments still due.

Research evidence has found a number of major factors that increase the risk of heart disease. They are: cigarette smoking, high blood pressure, high blood cholesterol levels, obesity and, by no means the least, lack of exercise. Discussion of the first four are covered in other books. Let's focus on that last one—lack of exercise.

Why this special emphasis on the heart? Because if you don't already realize it, your heart is *the single most important muscle* of the 600 muscles in your entire body. Most people neglect their hearts by not doing the proper exercises. Calisthenics, weight lifting, stretching classes just don't hack it. They don't provide cardiovascular fitness. Other people don't do any exercise at all. If you work your heart, it is going to work for you. Don't work it, and it will atrophy or waste away like any other muscle not used. Did you ever see a broken arm or leg just after the cast has been removed? Withered, shrunken and weak, those muscles must be exercised and strengthened slowly and carefully before they will return to normal size. That is the remarkable thing about the human body. Our bones, ligaments, joint cartilages and muscles have the ability to regenerate through exercise.

Most Americans eat too much, drink too much, smoke too much and, above all, sit too much. Which category do you fall into? More than one? All? We are soft, overweight, unable to perform at peak levels. We are prime candidates for an early retirement—from life! Our children are not in good shape. Our adult population is not in shape. Nor are our senior citizens. Well then, who is?

In a study taken a number of years ago comparing children of the United States to those of several European countries, it was found that the American children lagged far behind in physical conditioning. The school systems are to be blamed for not fostering enough interest in non-team sports, such as racewalking, bicycling, swimming, paddleball and handball, which can easily be followed in adult life. Although not fully substantiated but certainly worth mentioning are recent pronouncements by various doctors concerning longevity. Dr. Walter Bortz of the Stanford University Medical School says that "good nutrition, good exercise and good rest are the three elements of health. Coupled with an aggressive program of preventive medicine, they would add at least 10 years to the average American's lifespan."

In May 1973, the President's Council on Physical Fitness and Sports announced that 55 percent of Americans engaged in regular exercise. Late in 1977, a Gallup Poll found that only 47 percent of Americans exercised regularly. A decrease of 8 percent! Despite the physical fitness boom that we supposedly have been enjoying in the intervening years, we are actually doing less. What are we doing to ourselves? The ancient Romans had a saying, "Man does not die, he kills himself!" The trouble with us is that we are too sophisticated, too mechanized and too advanced in modern technology for our own good. We are becoming victims of our own inventions. The automobile is the worst thing to happen to walking. Our children, instead of walking blocks or miles to school, are now transported by car or bus. Before and after school and on weekends, they glue themselves to their television sets and you can't get them to move. And the adults are no better, driving to the store only a few blocks away, to get what —a pack of cigarettes! Despite all the warnings from the American Cancer Society—even with a federally legislated warning right on the pack—cigarette consumption persists.

Years ago rugs were taken out to the backyard and beaten with a stick or a paddle. Breads and cakes were hand mixed. Lawns were mowed by the pushing of a hand mower. There were no escalators and few elevators. Did you know that walking up stairs is a dynamic way to burn off calories, even more than is running? Years ago human muscles got plenty of use. People were in far better shape then than they are now. Our technology has been diabolically effective in eliminating physical activity from our daily pattern of living. Each "advance" in our style of living—the automobile, washing machine, oil furnace, television—has acted to diminish human activity —and our own physical well-being.

People used to work every day and rest on the Sabbath. Today, most people in this country work 5 days—Monday through Friday. Now there is talk, because of more automation, of a 4-day work week. What are we going to do with ourselves? We should consider that question carefully. The less physical activity we do, the less we will be able to do.

In as much as the need for physical activity in most occupations is about to be abolished, it will be necessary, even vital, to devote some considerable part of the leisure time to physical activity in order to maintain an optimal function of the body. Now, I'm not advocating beating your rugs by hand. Nor do I ask you to convert to coal and stoke the furnace yourself. What I am advocating is a regular exercise program to keep your body from deteriorating—putting you back into shape and keeping yourself that way. Exercise is just as necessary for life as the food we eat and the oxygen we breathe. We will not restore exercise to its proper role in our lives unless we really believe in its importance and understand its benefits.

Let us now look at how we can arrest some of the debilitating conditions of being physically inactive and how we can improve the quality of our lives and of our physical well-being. We will examine what true fitness is, how we can directly benefit from an exercise program, why it is important to continue it throughout life, and how we can come to enjoy and actually look forward to our training.

Just what does it mean to be physically fit? According to Dr. Lenore R. Zohman of Montefiore Hospital and Medical Center in New York, and a leading cardiologist:

> Physical fitness, actually cardiovascular fitness, is an observable and predictable benefit of exercise training. It is a state of body efficiency enabling a person to exercise vigorously for a long time period without fatigue and to respond to sudden physical and emotional demands with an economy of heartbeats and only a modest rise in blood pressure.

That individual has built up a measure of endurance and is able with less effort to supply more energy to the muscles so that they can work harder and longer. This puts less strain on the cardiovascular system (the heart and the vessels supplying it). Being in shape means a lowered pulse rate so that your heart does not have to work so hard at whatever you do. Blood pressure will be lowered. The serum triglyceride level will also be lowered—a hedge against atherosclerosis. Being fit reduces the tendency of the blood to form clots that could provoke a heart attack. The American Heart Association says that it is at least "prudent" to exercise because it can probably decrease your chances of having a heart attack or of having another if you have already been stricken. Furthermore, if you do have a heart attack at all, it will probably be milder if you are physically fit. Another benefit of exercise is the development of supplemental blood vessels to the heart, so that if a main vessel is blocked by a clot, the heart muscle will still receive oxygen.

So it should now be clear to you that besides the benefits described to you in the preceding chapter, the heart really takes top billing in what should receive special attention in exercising for fitness. But we cannot isolate the heart and work it by itself. We must *move* and *work* the systems that work and support the heart. In turn, they are supported by the heart. For the air that we breathe and the nutrients from our food to cleanse and enrich our bodies, we must do exercises that develop better circulation. In order to promote an optimal fitness level, the musculoskeletal, the cardiovascular and the cardiorespiratory systems must all work together in concert. Exercises that promote this level work the entire body, giving strength to the systems that support the heart as well as to the heart itself. You will increase your strength, coordination and endurance. You will have an improved ability to relax and voluntarily to reduce tension. You can, with proper diet, become slimmer and firmer. You will look better. You will feel better. It will change your life. But . . .

Being physically fit does not just happen to you. It takes *work!* And that is what this book is all about . . . how to work your body in a safe and reasonable manner so as to avoid injuring yourself—how to Racewalk to Fitness.

I assume that by now you have decided to join the team. For you new athletes, therefore, I have a fitness program formulated to develop optimal work efficiency. It is called the Coach's Racewalk Program. You will derive from it just what you put into it. But you will have to do it all yourself. A coach can guide, inspire, teach and encourage an athlete, but then the athlete must do the rest herself or himself.

You will begin to see and feel results rather quickly. Perhaps even as soon as a month. During the first couple of weeks, you may experience some minor muscle soreness because you have reawakened some lazy muscles, but that will quickly pass. You will develop an increase in your endurance level and an accompanying warm feeling of achievement. You may find that at the end of the day, you are less tired from your day at work than ever before. Your clothing may begin to feel loose. Not wanting to undo what good things you are doing for your body . . . you *will* refuse that extra helping of potatoes or bread that was passed to you. You will be proud of yourself and rightly so. The results will make work become pleasure. Dedication will be creeping into your head. So much so that you will look forward to your next Racewalk Training session.

This is a program that you can follow from the beginner level all the way through to the advanced stages of competitive racewalking. Except for competitive racewalking, it will be the easiest and safest program to adhere to and the one that will give you the most return for your investment—your time and effort. The Coach's Racewalk Program will keep you fitter, slimmer and younger looking for as long as you stay with it. The coaching that you receive from me now can put you in better shape than you have ever been. And you can be an "athlete in training" for the rest of your life.

Move! Put your heart into it.

O.K. YOU ARE CONVINCED
So What's Next?

Well, rest assured you are not going to go at it like "gangbusters." That's for sure. Now that you have opted for the life of an athlete—a racewalker—there are still some preliminaries which you will go through before you actually go out for your first workout. We will be discussing a medical examination, an abbreviated biomechanical checkup, and the qualifications of your doctor to give advice on exercise. You will also find out what to wear in all kinds of weather and possible sites for training. This section is like an orientation before starting a new summer camp, or a new school, or as you are doing—joining a new team in a sport that is new for you. But for you, racewalking could be a lifetime sport, an activity that may very well change and improve the quality of your life. So pay strict attention. Don't think that you can skim through this part before you get to the "good stuff"—about exercise and technique. Neglecting advice about doctors, footgear, clothing, etc., may cause you much discomfort and perhaps pain later on. Now let's get on with it.

Many of you who are in reasonably good health, with no adverse medical history and no symptoms that concern you, can probably start on the Program without a medical examination and have no feeling of discomfort. But I urge you now: Don't try to do too much too soon! Stay within the guidelines of the Program. Every one of you should have at least a checkup and/or consult with your family physician informing him that you are planning or beginning a training program. Here are a few aside comments on rating your doctor on exercise advice. Many doctors are in poor shape themselves so they are not going to be able to set an example for you. Most medical schools provide very little training in exercise physiology so they are not really going to be able to advise you about the specific benefits of exercising. Just have the necessary checkup, to be sure you're not asking for trouble, and obtain the clearance for participation in brisk walking as your form of exercise activity. After that, you will really be giving *yourself* the prescription for preventive medicine.

Now for some real words of caution: If you are over 35 or if you are *any age* and smoke heavily, are obese, have diabetes, or have a history of heart disease in your family, then I strongly recommend that you not only have a complete screening physical examination including a chest X-ray and an electrocardiogram but also an exercise stress electrocardiogram.

An electrocardiogram, EKG, records the electrical changes that take place in the heart while resting. Medical examinations that rely on rest electrocardiograms to assess the heart's condition can miss dangerous changes. Dr. Kenneth Cooper, who popularized the aerobic concept of fitness, compares the exercise stress electrocardiogram to the road test a person might give a used car he or she contemplates buying. Just listening to an idling engine certainly won't tell you as much about the car as a road test where the engine is accelerated and runs at high speed for a period of time. Most doctors now believe that the heart must be tested in the same way before it can be certified as sound. Certain performance levels according to age, sex and physical condition have been established. The stress test starts with the individual beginning to exercise slowly, and then gradually increasing effort. The heart's performance is charted and compared with that of a normal heart of the same age and sex. The value of the stress test, therefore, is twofold. First, it measures the heart's working capability, clearing a fit individual for sustained exercise. Second, it can be used to establish exercise limits for those individuals whose hearts are deficient and who need rehabilitation. But before you make any appointment with just any testing center, be forewarned. Stress testing has become one of the most popular and fashionable medical procedures in America. Everybody is looking to get into the act. Make sure that your test will be given by a cardiologist whose assistants are trained in the administration of such tests. Also make sure that they have on hand—visible to all—a fully equipped emergency resuscitation kit. Ask! Don't be shy! Dr. Cooper reports that the possibility of overworking a deficient heart during the test is extremely rare but it does exist. At his center only four incidents, none fatal, occurred in 16,500 stress tests.

Another reason for my recommending a medical examination is for you to avoid certain foot problems before they occur. Almost *no one* goes to a podiatrist *before* beginning a training program. The occasion when the podiatrist sees you is *after* you have developed an injury. If you were to have a podiatric examination beforehand, you could avoid many injuries by enabling your doctor to locate any structural imbalance or biomechanical problems that may require some correction before you begin. Otherwise, you are cleared to train.

What to wear, or the various pieces of equipment that you'll need, is really no big deal. And certainly no cause for a lot of concern. Walking requires no major investment in equipment, other than a reasonably good pair of training shoes. The clothing that you wear to work around the house or to play touch football with the kids— "knock-around clothes"—is fine. After a month or two of training and seeing what good progress you have made, if you want to reward yourself with an item of athletic gear such as a warm-up suit or track shorts or singlet . . . do it! You will by then be an athlete, so wear what the athletes wear. Just make sure that it is comfortable.

If you live in an area where there are extreme changes in the weather, dress for the weather and use your common sense. You will learn quickly enough just how much to wear. I will share with you some of my "weather-wise" tips from 35 years of training in all kinds of weather. A basic concept that I always adhere to is that of layered dressing. That is, many (or few) layers of light clothing so that the dead air trapped between the layers acts as insulation to keep the body warm. Your body will generate a lot of heat when you exercise. Even when you train in bitter cold weather, you won't have to dress as warmly as you would have to for normal activities such as going to work or shopping.

Here, then, are my notes on the various gear that you will need or might like to have for walking.

Shoes

Because the interest in physical fitness has created technologically superior training shoes, they are much better for your feet than street shoes or some old pair of canvas sneakers or boat shoes that you might have lying around your closet. My advice, therefore, is to buy a pair as soon as you can. Prices range from $15 and up, but they are worth the expense.

Comfort, fit and protection are the key points to look for in a training shoe. Forget the fashion approach. Forget style and colors. Don't make the same mistakes that many of you make when you buy a pair of street or dress shoes. You are not buying them for a fashion show.

Choose a sporting goods store or shoe store that carries as wide a selection as possible. You will want the opportunity to try on a number of different brands because each gives you a slightly different fit. Ask for a training shoe. Don't let anyone sell you a beautiful pair of racing flats! They don't offer enough support.

Good cushioning is a necessity for prevention of muscle and joint soreness, which often leads to injury. Support from built-in arches, rigid shanks and well-contoured uppers, which hold the foot in place directly over the soles, are the requisites of good training shoes.

Look for a shoe with a midsole, a heel wedge that is medium firm (it should be approximately ½ inch thick), and a durable, thick and

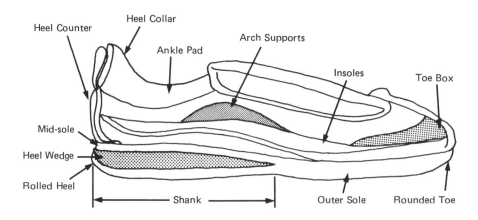

reasonably flexible outer sole. The shoe should have a stable wide heel and should be flexible at its widest point—the ball of the foot where it bends as you push off with each stride. Take the shoe in your hands and bend it. If it doesn't bend easily, ask for a different style. Now check the shank. As shown in the diagram, the shank constitutes the sole from the front of the arch back to the heel. The shank should be quite rigid for true support. Now check the top of the shoe, first looking at the heel counter, which is the back of the shoe cupping your heel. It should have a firm and stable plastic or fiber inner liner with leather outer counter material. The shoe should have insoles, a built-in arch support (usually a rubber insert), ankle pads and a heel collar. The toe box should be high and wide to allow natural toe spread. This conforms more closely to the general shape of the foot, which reduces blistering and allows a better fit.

Bring with you or ask for a pair of thick sweat socks. Most stores have them available for those who know they are going to wear them while training. Put both shoes on, lace them both all the way, and stand up. Don't remain seated. It is not a true test of fit. You should be able to wiggle your toes slightly, and your big toe should be about ½ inch to ¾ inch from the tip of the shoe. The laces should be drawn so that you feel the arch support and snug feeling from the soles to the laces on each side of your foot. The heel should be cupped snugly; you should not be able to lift your heel out of the shoe while the bottom of the heel is held on the floor. *Don't* settle for less than a good fit.

Athletic shoes generally run a half size larger than your street shoe size. I really don't want to get into brand names, but with respect to fit I will make a couple of observations. Adidas has a tendency to fit a slightly narrower foot well. Puma, Nike and Tiger fit slightly wider feet well. Brooks and New Balance offer shoes in both wide and narrow widths.

Shoes with nylon uppers require very little break-in period and are lighter in weight than leather. Nylon takes less care since it does not harden or crack from repeated wetness, and it dries quickly. There are some shoes with nylon mesh uppers that are cool in summer. I like them but I put them away during winter. Some people wash their nylon shoes in the washing machine because they smell. After a workout I simply let mine air out, then spray them. I won't put mine in the wash. You won't have that problem if you buy shoes with leather or suede uppers but you'll have another. Leather and suede ᴦan give a closer fit, but if they crack forget it. If my shoes get really wet in the rain or from puddles, I stuff paper toweling in them and let them dry, away from the heat. There are patch kits with goo which you can use to prolong the tips and heels of your shoes. Many athletic shoe stores have repair services. If the uppers are in good shape, depending upon the original cost of the shoe, you might want to have them resoled. The price is about $14–$15, so you'll have to decide if it's worth it.

When you buy your shoes, buy an extra pair of laces on the spot. As good as the shoe may be, laces just don't hold up. Keep a small washcloth or hand towel to wipe off your shoes and a plastic bag in which to put them when you travel. If you are going to train in wet weather and you have leather uppers, you can put a thin smear of Vaseline on them and wipe it off later. It doesn't work with suede.

A word about changing shoe models: Don't do it unless you are unhappy about the shoe you have now. You don't know how much trouble you can cause yourself if you get a pair that is not right for you. A comfortable shoe is a really good friend.

Socks

Socks or what kind or no socks is a very individual thing. It is a question of comfort. I think that most of you will be most comfortable with a pair of anklet sweat socks, either Orlon or wool. Some of the women might prefer a thin cotton anklet. The tennis people have come up with half socks. There are two reasons that necessitate the use of a sock. First, to reduce any abrasion from the shoe and second, to absorb perspiration. Make sure that the sock fits snugly on your foot, with no holes or wrinkles or lumps that can cause blisters. Some people like the feeling of freedom and can't stand the weight of socks, especially when they get wet. Some of this you will have to experiment with yourself. In the winter you can rest assured you will want to wear socks. Sometimes, although rarely, it is so cold that I use the layering principle even on my feet. I wear a thin pair of nylon dress socks underneath my heavy sweat socks. Toasty warm.

Shirts

The best all-purpose shirt is the T-shirt, preferably cotton because it better absorbs the perspiration. I wear a T-shirt when the temperature is between 55°F and 75°F. Above that I take it off or cut the sleeves from it or wear a sleeveless vest, commonly called an athletic singlet, like sleeveless underwear. When the temperature is between 45° to 55°F I usually wear a long-sleeved cotton turtleneck under the T-shirt. For temperatures in the 20s I wear a light nylon jacket under my warm-up jacket but over the turtleneck and the T-shirt. The nylon jacket (skiers call it a wind shirt) is the third layer, and I think it keeps the body heat in better than when used as the outermost garment. At 5°F below zero I usually add, underneath, an Orlon or old wool turtleneck that I have and I am warm. You can find out for yourself by trying different combinations of layering. If you are a bit too warm, you can always loosen your jacket or take it off and tie it around your waist. Don't be a hero or heroine and go out without being properly dressed for the cold weather. A sudden wind, a sudden chill and you are flat on your back with a thermometer sticking out of your mouth. You can always peel off a layer or two, but if you don't have it on to begin with . . . doctor bills.

Shorts and Pants and Underpants

Muscles work better and have fewer chances for pulling when they are warm. I wear my warm-up suit for training in all temperatures up to 50°F. You can wear a pair of slacks, jeans, corduroys, chinos— whatever. That is, unless you decide to buy a warm-up suit. No, it is not a necessity. But they are available in all price ranges now and some of them look pretty sharp. When the weather gets colder, like below freezing, I put on a pair of long underwear pants under my warm-ups. Underneath them both, I wear a pair of nylon track shorts. They now come with their own built-in underpants. They provide adequate support and are quite comfortable. They even have a small pocket for keys and money. The cut is such that they can be worn by men or women. I like them because they are lightweight and cool and dry easily. I don't like jockey shorts because with vigorous walking, I find that they ride up my behind. Some women have voiced this complaint as well. Consequently, some women wear swimming trunks made of nylon. They are close fitting and are worn without underwear. Above 50°F the long johns and sweat pants come off, and I train in shorts for most of the spring, summer and fall. There are plenty of styles of cotton athletic shorts and tennis shorts, or you can even train in cut-off jeans. As long as you are comfortable and use common sense . . . that's what counts.

Brassieres and Jocks

Many small breasted women train without a bra. Most larger breasted women prefer training with a bra for comfort and support. Then there are women who will always wear a bra whether they really need one or not. The number one choice of most women is a one-size, over-the-head bra, copied from a French import, that is of stretch nylon and has no hooks or metal clips. This bra practically eliminates any irritation or friction. Really large breasted women wear a regular bra because they need the support, so they put a piece of tape on their skin, under the clip to avoid abrasion. A new bra has been introduced, called a sport bra. There is not enough feedback to rate it yet. Men don't really have much of a choice. It is either a pair of shorts with a built-in supporter or jockey shorts or a jock. Incidentally, the best type of jock is a nylon one with a 1-inch waistband that won't curl.

Caps

Most people can go bareheaded most of the time except during cold weather or in a brutally hot sun. When the temperature is cold enough to nip at your ears, that's the time to put on a wool or Orlon knitted cap. It has been estimated that close to 40 percent of lost body heat escapes through your head, so cover up that "release valve" in winter and you'll stay warmer. Some summer days the sun really blazes down on you, especially if you're going to be out for a long time. A baseball cap, golf cap, an old tennis cap, even a handkerchief tied at the four corners will do the trick to protect your head from the direct sun.

Gloves

My hands get especially cold at anything below 40°F. At that point I wear my cheap cotton gardening gloves, which I throw into the laundry every week. (They also double as a nose brusher in cold, leaky-nose weather.) When it gets colder I switch to wool gloves, and when it's really cold I add a pair of sweat socks over the gloves. If your hands start to perspire, take them off and carry them for a while or tuck them in the waistband of your pants.

Care of Your Clothing

Federal law dictates having care labels attached to clothing, but many times they either fall off or become entirely illegible through repeated washings. In my own case the labels are sometimes stiff and scratchy against my skin so I simply cut them off. I stick to cold-water washings for all of my items and avoid the problems of colors bleeding. Wash your training gear often. You might want to look like an athlete, but you don't have to smell like the whole locker room. Besides, salt-encrusted items next to your skin tend to chafe.

Other Kinds of Stuff

A wristwatch with a sweep-second hand is probably the most important training aid you can use, especially in the beginning of the program. Since your arm movement will be vigorous, a wristwatch with an expansion bracelet jiggles around too much. Try a nylon or vinyl strap with air holes.

Usually the warm-up suit has a pocket or two; it's the shorts that may not. You can sew a patch pocket on the outside or inside, maybe 3 inches by 3 inches, or you can make a small pouch in which you can carry keys and some money. I usually carry a dime or two to make phone calls, a couple of quarters in case I want to buy a soda, and a few dollars if I want to buy some fruit or groceries on the way home.

Fold up a good-sized length of toilet paper and put it in a pocket or tuck it in the waistband of your shorts. When you are on a long workout, you may very well have to duck into the bushes so never be without it.

Vaseline is another must. Apply a smear to the inside of your thighs and under the elastic of underwear or a jock or where the built-ins will rub. You may need some at the back of your underarm because of your vigorous arm movement. If I am going out for a long workout, I carry a glob folded up in a piece of aluminum foil and keep it in my pouch. Sometimes you have to apply a bit more once you're well into the workout. Also, during a long workout you may have to put Vaseline or a square of adhesive tape or a Band-Aid over your nipples to protect them from abrasion. Your shirt will constantly rub against them, especially when it is wet from perspiration.

Many people leave their glasses home when they go out for a workout. Don't! This imperative has nothing to do with safety. At the speed at which you will be walking, you can really get into your surroundings, whether you walk the city streets or the open country roads. You can enjoy people watching, bird watching (really watch out for those dogs), and just taking it all in—enjoying. When I go for a really long walk on a scenic route, I take along a lightweight camera and take some pictures. Even though I take my training very seriously, I do make time for other pursuits. Some people carry small radios or headsets when they go for a long workout. I don't because I cherish that time spent alone with my thoughts.

Where to Racewalk

The simplest answer to where to racewalk is just about anywhere! That is the beauty of walking for exercise. You don't need any special facilities or equipment.

In the beginning of your program, you can just open your front door and start walking. Whether you live in the city, the suburbs or the country, your initial walks will be from 20 to 30 minutes—so you can start by walking around the block or set an out-and-back course for yourself. Walk out for 10 or 15 minutes—say—downtown. When the 10 or 15 minutes are up, turn around and head for home. As you become accustomed to your pace and as you begin to increase the time spent training, expand your horizons. If you feel like it, change your course to explore new neighborhoods or sites. If you find a beautiful scenic path and you really enjoy it, you will begin to know every stone, every turn, every animal along the way. Take those moments to get into yourself, to meditate, to be alone with yourself. Stick with that workout site if you really love it. That can be your special place and your special time. I have a favorite early morning workout path along the East River Drive. I start out when it is pitch black. Soon a faint tinge of pink starts to glow in the east. Shortly afterward the sun rises and shines bright yellow, bouncing across the water, brightening everything and warming me. Money can't buy such good feelings.

TWO

Here's How

5

THE SCIENCE OF BREATHING

Without breath there is no life. That is a fundamental fact of life which we take so much for granted—until our breath is threatened. Being choked or smothered will quickly snuff out a life. Dive deep in the water and see how fast you try to surface, gasping for breath. Acrid fumes of smoke will send you frantically searching for air. How about a long kiss with a stuffy nose? Right? When we think about it we have really known all along the importance of breathing and of breathing good quality air. What we have forgotten is *how* to breathe properly in order to have that air do its vital work on all the millions of cells in our bodies. Proper breathing can help to eliminate depression, poor digestion, colds and a sallow complexion. It will enrich your blood with life-sustaining oxygen that will improve your vitality and alertness, allowing you to sleep better and play better.

Primitive man didn't need any instruction in breathing. Neither does the animal. Watch babies in their cribs. Babies breathe so naturally. Their stomachs rise as they inhale, and they sleep peacefully with their mouths closed. They inhale through their noses, stomachs expanding, and exhale again through their noses, stomachs flattening. This, the natural way to breathe, is called diaphragmatic or belly breathing. When I was a child the physical education instructors used to say to us, "Stand straight, deep breath, suck in your stomach!" In the Army they say, "Stand tall, deep breath, suck in your stomach, chest out!" *Wrong!* Most people are very shallow breathers, breathing from the upper chest only. As a coach, I have trained myself to look mostly for what is *wrong* with an athlete's technique, not so much at what is right. As the flaws are corrected, the efficiency increases and the performances improve. Many times during a training workout I focus only on one element of a technique for a while, observing what people are doing. One thing that I see quite often is the lack of proper breathing. All that puffing, gasping and wheezing is so wrong and so unnecessary. They are breathing shallowly, robbing their systems of oxygen. Shortly, I will teach you diaphragmatic or belly breathing.

Bur first, it would be helpful for us to go over some basic biology of the organs of respiration, which consist of the two lungs and the air passages leading to them. In normal breathing, air enters the respiratory system through the nostrils. The nostrils have a few hairs just inside the entrance, which act as filters to catch any coarse particles that may be floating in the air. The nose and the entire respiratory tract are lined with ciliated (hairlike) epithilial cells and mucous membranes. These hairlike cells all beat in rhythm toward the exits to remove irritating particles and mucus. This lining is kept moist by the secretions of gobletlike cells in the mucous membranes. The mucous membranes are also richly supplied with blood, warming the air on contact. Leading off from the nasal passages are four pairs of hollows called sinuses which further warm and clean the air. Air passing through thus far has been cleaned, warmed and moistened. The air continues back and down the windpipe, which branches into two tubes called bronchi, each leading to a separate lung. The bronchi subdivide within each lung like the branches of a tree. This subdivision continues into tiny branches called bronchioles. Each tiny bronchiole terminates in tiny air sacs called alveoli. Every human body contains approximately 600 million alveoli and if spread out, their entire surface area would be twenty-four times that of the whole body. The lungs are like a multicellular sponge, soaking up the air on inhalation and squeezing it out on exhalation. Now we can begin to recognize the importance of the diaphragm. It is this strong, flat, sheetlike muscle stretched across the chest under the lungs that, upon expanding, increases the size of the lungs, allowing the air to rush into the vacuum thus created. The deeper the inhalation, the better chance for the air to reach into these millions of air sacs. It is in the millions of air cells in the lungs that a form of combustion takes place when the blood returning from the body, laden with waste products from all parts of the system, mixes with the fresh oxygen and releases carbon dioxide gas. An exchange takes place whereby the blood is now purified and carried back to the heart. The gas and impure air are expelled from the system upon exhalation. The heart can now pump rich, red and clean blood to all parts of the system.

If the blood is not fully purified by this regenerative process of the lungs, it returns to the arteries containing waste products and without its full share of life-giving oxygen. It certainly does not make sense to be recycling residue-laden blood through your system when you can breathe properly and supply the body with rich, clean blood. The blood also absorbs a quantity of oxygen and carries it to each and every cell, tissue, muscle and organ in your body, oxygenating and revitalizing them. Lack of sufficient oxygen can also prevent your digestive processes from functioning properly, robbing the body of the nutritive benefits of the food you eat.

As you can see, it is not just for exercise that you need to breathe properly. It is vital to your whole being. Just to get the idea, try:

The Basic Diaphragmatic Breathing Exercise

1. Lie on the floor on your back with your knees bent and feet comfortably apart (6–8 inches). Have your shoulders, hips, knees and ankles aligned as shown. The lower back, shoulders and the back of the neck should be pressed toward the floor. Relaxing completely, inhale through your nose to a count of 4. Fill up your stomach only. P–U–S–H up with your stomach muscles.

2. Now slowly exhale to a count of 8, gently contracting your rib.cage and then your abdomen. When you feel that you have exhausted all the air, use your muscles to pull your abdomen in toward your spine and hold for a 2 count. Repeat 6 times.

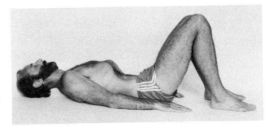

THE IMPORTANCE OF WARM-UP

Special note from your coach:

I separate a training session into three segments: the warm-up, the workout, and the cool-down. Each segment has its own importance. The sum total of how you work in each of these segments will determine whether or not you have had a good training session.

An intelligent athlete will listen to the advice of his or her coach. Whether you were an athlete and are on the comeback trail or you want to become an athlete and want to put your body in shape, *don't become a casualty!* Listen to your coach! I cannot emphasize enough the importance of a proper warm-up. Tight muscles will not perform well. Long, lean, elastic muscles will do the job. Face it, you are out of shape. You must prepare your body for each workout just as you should warm up the car engine on a cold day before driving away.

The connective tissues that make up ligaments, tendons and parts of muscles are less elastic because of your inactivity. Under stress they are subject to partial and even major tears. Breathing and stretching exercises will warm your "engine" by stretching the muscle-tendon units, increase their actual temperature, and give you flexibility to perform with less chance for injury.

Doing the warm-up exercises before your workout and the special few designated for the cool-down, in the next chapter, should keep you from the ranks of the "walking wounded"—those who did too much too soon.

CAUTION: TRAINING WITHOUT A WARM-UP MAY BE INJURIOUS TO YOUR BODY.

7

PREKINETICS
Five Thousand Years of Experience

Modern man has walked upright for more than half a million years. Walking is man's oldest means of transportation. The oldest recorded science of physical and mental health is that of Yoga, which was developed in India well over 5,000 years ago. There are no forms of exercise more fitting than Yoga-based exercises to complement man's oldest exercise—walking. The yogis discovered that certain physical postures would stretch, strengthen and cleanse the muscles if done slowly, remaining in the posture for a period of time, and breathing deeply. The increased circulation due to the exercise and the oxygenated blood energize and purify the system.

Prekinetics, taken from the Greek *before movement,* are a series of breathing and flexibility exercises based on yoga postures, adapting the best features of this Eastern discipline to the sports-conscious Western world. As yoga means unity or "getting in touch with one's self," with *Prekinetics* you will learn to tune in on your mind and body during your warm-up. By closing your eyes and concentrating on certain postures, you can relax more and feel the stretch. By concentration, you will open up your mind so that it will be receptive to your body. It can be a period of meditation where you turn inward, discovering your areas of tension, weakness and strength. Then, while holding the pose and relaxing, and breathing deeply, you will gain strength, flexibility and energy. These postures, together with deep breathing, are so designed as to stretch your muscles, stimulate your body organs, and literally pour glandular chemicals and oxygen into your bloodstream to prepare you for your workout.

If you were to go to a ballet studio before a class, you would see dancers sprawled all over the floors and hallways, bending and stretching. They have known for years the value of warming up, of preparing themselves just as much for a class as for a performance.

Too many of the physical training teachers, coaches and instructors are still coaching today with ideas of yesterday. Most typical of their latter-day philosophy is that it has to hurt to be doing any good. They still give calisthenic exercises as a warm-up before a workout. Some calisthenics are strength builders. They are good. But most are ballistic (bouncing) type exercises that tend to force the stretch, causing pain. Most people are told, "Push, touch your toes." The pain that these participants feel from forcing is the pain of contracted muscles trying to be stretched. This overstretching happens too often, injuring the muscle fibers. Exercise physiologists and some enlightened coaches have only recently "discovered" what the yogis have been saying for 5,000 years. Yoga advocates slow, easy stretching, only to the edge of pain, whatever your edge may be. For example, you may assume a pose with your feet together, knees straight, and bending from the waist, try to grasp your ankles. In yoga, if you cannot grasp your ankles, simply grasp your leg at whatever point you begin to feel tension, even if it is only at your knees. That day, that is your edge. With continued exercise—easy stretching and breathing "into" the posture so that you remain relaxed and the oxygen is able to feed those working cells—you will stretch your muscle-tendon units millimeter by millimeter, continually moving your "edge" until you feel no tension and no pain at all. That's because muscle tissue has the unique property of contractability.

Prekinetics are specifically designed to align your body. With proper alignment, your muscles will be stretched and strong. Your joints will have full range of motion, and energy will flow equally to all parts of your body. You will be able to train knowing that you have "bought your insurance" toward preventing injuries such as a pulled muscle or a torn ligament. Your increased range of motion will enable you to move freely and easily.

You may learn to enjoy, as I do, the benefit of doing your stretching barefoot. Most podiatrists advocate going without shoes and socks as much as possible, especially on more yielding surfaces such as carpets, grass or sand. The ancient Greek warriors and athletes trained in sand to build up the musculature of the feet. Foot doctors also prescribe wiggling and rotating the feet while seated in order to maintain muscle tone and circulation for standing and other activities. Ever since I was a kid I have enjoyed the feeling of walking barefoot. When I do my exercises I have a better feeling of stability and of contact with the ground. My toes grip the carpet better. I feel my energy better. And when I warm up on grass, I feel that the energy from the whole earth is transmitted through my feet into my body. Try it. You will kick off your shoes whenever you can.

As busy as you may be with your family, occupation, social commitments and other interests, you must take the precaution to take a complete *Prekinetics* warm-up before you go out and train. Don't make the mistake of hurrying through your warm-up or of cutting it short. If time becomes a problem, cut the *workout* short or increase your pace (but only after you have reached the intermediate level). The following pages show the complete *Prekinetics* warm-up routine which can be accomplished in 15–20 minutes.

The exercises themselves and their sequence are choreographed to tune up your breathing, increase your pulse rate, stimulate your circulation, increase your body temperature, loosen up your muscles and heighten your awareness. Specific muscle groups will be stretched and strengthened in order to prepare you best for a race-walking training session.

After your workout, do the special cool-down exercises as prescribed. Any tightness or aches will be helped by this specially prepared sequence, allowing you to cool down comfortably and finally to relax. Be sure you take the time for them. Remember you do your warm-up exercises for today's workout. You do your cool-down exercises for *tomorrow's* workout.

You might want to consider doing a *Prekinetics* routine before you play tennis, basketball, football, racquetball, swimming or any other sport. I have participated individually and have played on various teams in the above sports and I always do. I marvel at how some athletes avoid warm-up exercises like they would the plague.

If you become a believer, as I have, then you too will spread the word:

DON'T TRAIN WITHOUT A WARM-UP!
DON'T STRAIN IN YOUR WARM-UP!
NO STRAIN. NO PAIN.

Prekinetics—*Before the Workout*

The Top Twenty Exercises to Prepare You for Your Workout

BELLY BREATHING

The lifting of the abdomen strengthens the diaphragm and the abdominal muscles. It stretches the lower lobes of the lungs, increases circulation and promotes hormonal secretions. It helps with digestion and stimulates sluggish elimination, and is an excellent strengthener for "forcing" your breathing during a fast pace.

1. With feet apart at shoulder width, place your hands just above your knees. Inhale deeply through your nose, pushing your stomach out.

2. Now force the air out through your mouth with a strong "haa" sound. Tighten your rib cage and stomach as you exhale, getting the last bit of air out. Holding your breath, try to suck in your stomach even more—toward the back of the spine. Hold for 10 seconds without breathing.

3. Relax and repeat 3 times.

LUNG POWER

This exercise really opens up your chest, allowing air to come into the apex (upper portion) of your lungs. You will also work your upper back, shoulders, chest and arms by applying resistance during the exercise.

1. With feet apart at shoulder width, clasp your hands with arms straight in front of you. Inhale deeply through your nose, pushing your stomach out.

2. As you inhale, also raise your clasped hands overhead while holding your breath for 15 to 20 seconds.

3. Lower your hands behind your neck, continually applying resistance as if you have to force them down. After the 20 seconds, exhale, pulling in your stomach, and place your hands at your sides.

4. Relax and repeat 3 times.

You may feel a "rush" or feel light-headed. You are experiencing a new breathing sensation.

HEAD ROLLS

These are excellent for relieving tension buildup in the neck and for tension headaches. The rolling motion also helps stimulate the thyroid gland which regulates the metabolism. These can be done while standing or sitting, as long as you keep your spine straight. Move as slowly as you can.

1. Keeping your shoulders down and breastbone lifted, allow your chin to sink down to your chest.

2. Inhale while rolling your head to the right so your right ear is parallel to your right shoulder.

3. Roll your head straight back, stretching your chin upward. Keep your shoulders down and relaxed. Don't let them shrug up toward your head.

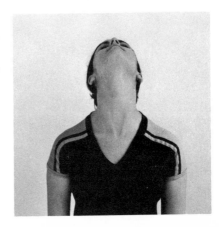

4. Exhale while rolling your head down toward your left shoulder. Feel the stretch on the opposite side of your neck. Roll down so your chin is again on your chest.

5. Do this exercise 3 times to the right and 3 times to the left.

KNEE BENDS

The knee is the largest joint in your body and plays a significant role in your locomotion. It is a delicate and temperamental instrument that should be warmed up well. This exercise departs from the traditional and often injurious deep knee bends, lessening stress on the joint itself by not putting the body's weight on the knee. It also imparts a good stretch to the hamstrings and lower back.

1. With toes, heels and knees together, squat down, placing fingers on the floor.

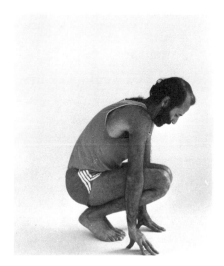

2. Inhale and straighten knees, leaving fingers on the floor. Only your legs are straightening. Your head and arms are stationary.

3. Exhale and go back to the squatting position.

4. Repeat 4–6 times or until really loose.

ACHILLES AND CALF STRETCH

The muscles of the calf fuse to form the Achilles tendon. The soleus muscle, which lies underneath the calf, is largely responsible for your propulsion. These are extremely important stretches and should be done a couple of times a day, wherever you are.

1. Stand about 3–4 feet from a wall or other support like a pole or tree. Lean against the wall, bending your arms as for a push-up, or clasp your hands and lean with your forearms. Bend your left leg and keep your right leg behind you as support. Move your hips forward until you feel the stretch on your right calf. Remember to keep your right heel on the floor. Hold for 15–20 seconds.

2. Now, still keeping the right heel on the floor, bend the right knee so that you feel the stretch in your Achilles. Hold for 15–20 seconds.

3. Reverse and do the left leg in the same manner.

QUAD STRETCH

This position stretches the quadriceps (front of the thigh) muscles. When done properly, the stretch is felt at the upper part of the thigh near the hip. It's an excellent stretch for increasing leg extension.

1. Stand erect, holding on to a chair or rail or wall. Bend your knee so that you can grasp your foot, and hold the heel against your butt. Now gently push back your knee as far as it will go. The push must be done by your leg. The hand just keeps the heel in place. Hold for 10 seconds.

2. Reverse your stance and do the other leg.

BACK BEND

With this exercise, the vertebral column is stretched and strengthened, the abdominal muscles stretched and toned, and the lung capacity increased. The lower back muscles are also strengthened.

1. Stand straight with your thighs and feet close together.

2. Breathe in deeply, raising the arms overhead; reach up and back. Push the hips forward and tighten the buttocks.

3. Hold for 10 seconds and release.

If you feel tension in the lower back, come up a bit.

INVERTED V

This exercise is good for upper body flexibility, especially the upper arms and shoulders. It is a mild stretch for the hamstrings inserting into the knees, an excellent stretch for the calves and the Achilles. It will tone up the lower end of the spine and the sciatic nerves.

1. On hands and knees, bring your hands even with and under your shoulders. Place your toes, heels and knees together.

2. Inhale and raise your hips high, to form an inverted V. Push your heels and armpits toward the floor. Feel the same push on the arms as on the legs. Tilt your behind toward the ceiling.

3. Breathe into the position. Hold for 20 seconds.

THE COBRA

The muscles in the small of the back are also necessary for good posture. This exercise strengthens them. The stretch gets at the chin line, the chest and the abdominals.

1. Lie face down on the floor with your toes pointed behind you, your heels together and your forehead flat on the floor. Place your hands just under your shoulders, keeping the elbows close to your sides.

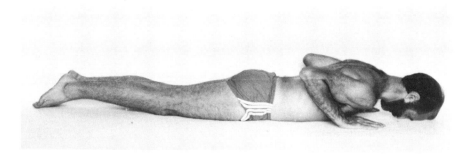

2. Tighten your buttocks, inhale, and slowly raise up by first lifting your head and shoulders off the floor without use of your hands. Stop and hold for a second or two while you exhale. Now as you inhale again, press your arms straight and tilt and push your chin up and back. Remember to keep your buttocks tight.

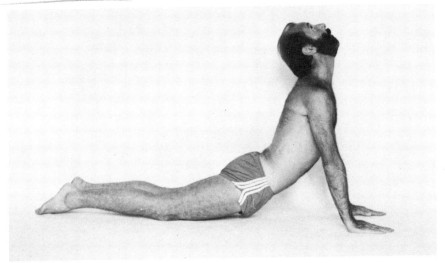

3. Hold for 10 seconds, or 20 if you feel comfortable. Come down slowly.

If you feel strain in the small of your back, spread your legs about a foot apart.

SIDE STRETCH

This is one of very few exercises that involve a sideways stretch of the spine, stimulating the spinal nerves. The muscles of the shoulder and side, the trunk-hip connection and the intercostals, which connect the ribs and are so vital to breathing, all get a good stretch. This posture is also slimming to the waist.

1. Stand with feet apart, one arm at your side, and raise the other arm. Inhale.

2. Exhale and leading with your head and the tips of the fingers, bend sideways, keeping your hips squared to the front. Knees and arms are kept straight. Slide your other hand toward your knee. Inhale.

3. Exhale and stretch farther. Don't twist your back. Keep both shoulders and hips squared. Reach out with the upper hand. Breathe and hold for 15 seconds.

4. Release and repeat on your other side.

TWIST

The twist stretches and loosens up the hips, the shoulders and the rib cage.

1. Stand with feet apart at a little more than shoulder width. Arms should be pushing outward, separating the shoulder blades.

2. Inhale, keeping the hips squared to the front, twist your head, body and arms as far to the right as they will go. Exhale and turn to front.

3. Repeat 2 times for each side.

BEND AND TWIST

This is an excellent stretch for the backs of the legs, the lower and upper back, and the arms.

1. Stand with feet apart at a little more than shoulder width. Arms should be pushing outward, separating the shoulder blades. Inhale.

2. Exhale and while keeping a flat back, bend from the waist. Arms remain spread. Inhale.

3. Exhale and keeping knees straight, reach across to grasp your left ankle with your right hand. Twist your body farther left and reach up with your left arm. Twist your head to look up at your left hand. Breathe while in the position. Hold for 15 seconds.

4. Release, come up, and do your right side.

BACK AND FORTH

This exercise limbers the spine and increases strength in your lower back. In the backward pose, the front thigh muscles are greatly strengthened. In the forward pose, the hamstrings get a good stretch and the lower back a great stretch. You'll feel it in your upper arms and shoulders. Blood flows to the brain and the central nervous system is stimulated.

1. Inhale, bend your knees forward just to maintain your balance. Leading with the head, bend backward and hold for 5 seconds.

2. Exhale and bend forward, knees straight, out over your legs and down.

3. Breathe in the position and hold for 10 seconds.

4. Grasp your leg or ankle and gently pull your head between your legs.

5. Breathe in the position and hold for 10 seconds.

HEAD TO KNEE

Again we emphasize the hamstring muscles. This also strengthens the upper arms and shoulders.

1. Standing with feet apart at shoulder width, turn out your left foot to about a 45-degree angle. Inhale.

2. Now exhale and bend from the waist with your head toward your knee. Try to straighten your arms toward the vertical position. Hold for 15 seconds. Breathe in the position.

3. Relax and do your right side.

THE EXTENSION STRETCH

The most important benefit of this position is that it increases stride length by stretching the pelvic area and the tops of the thighs. When you reach upward you not only increase the stretch, but you then stretch the abdominals and "open up" your chest cavity.

1. Take a long step back with your right leg, and hold your arms out for balance. Both feet should be pointed straight ahead.

2. Keeping your back straight and hips squared off, begin to "sit" forward until your left knee is over your toes. Raise your arms overhead.

3. Tuck your pelvis in and let gravity do some of the work. Sit farther down, keeping the front knee over the toes. Breathe into the position and hold for 20 seconds.

4. Relax and do your other side.

DEEP GROIN AND BUTTOCKS

This position really works on a hard-to-get-to area and imparts a good stretch.

1. Take a long step back with your right leg, and hold your arms out for balance. Both feet should be pointed straight ahead. Drop your right knee to the floor. Inhale.

2. Place your right hand next to your left foot and your left hand behind your back with your palm up. Exhale and move your left shoulder inside your left knee, bend your right arm and push down with your head toward the floor. Breathe in the position. Hold for 20–30 seconds.

3. Relax and do your other side.

(The left groin area is in the blind side of this picture, but it is the best angle for understanding the position.)

SQUAT STRETCH

This is another position especially good for the hard-to-get-at groin muscles. The position of the elbows inside the knee is the key. By completely relaxing and breathing deeply, then pulling the hands in closer to the body, you will be pushing the knees apart. Be gentle. It's also good for the lower back, the Achilles tendons and the pectoral muscles.

1. With your feet apart at shoulder width and slightly turned out, squat down.

2. Place your palms together, and with elbows braced against the knees, gently pull your palms to you. Deep breathing and complete relaxation is a must.

3. Hold for 20–30 seconds.

GROIN STRETCH

Here's one more for the hard-to-get-at area that needs attention. Be sure to keep your back straight as you bend into the position.

1. Stand with your feet apart a foot beyond each shoulder. Turn your left leg to about a 45-degree angle. Inhale. Interlock your thumbs in front.

2. Exhale and bend your left knee, keeping your right foot in its position. Keep your balance with your arms. Press the right hip down in order to intensify the stretch. Breathe into the position. Hold for 15 seconds.

3. Relax and do the other side.

HIP STRETCH

This position gets at the high hip. It looks simple, but you really have to feel for the maximum stretch.

1. Stand with feet apart at shoulder width.

2. Place your hands, one over the other, just above your right knee. Push against your hands and against your left hip at the same time. Now push your pelvis forward and sideward to feel the stretch. Breathe into it and hold for 15–20 seconds.

3. Relax and do your other side.

CADENCE BREATHING

You learned earlier about breathing, so now we will begin really to put it to work. Synchronize your arm action with your breathing. Allow your stomach to expand upon inhaling and contract upon exhaling.

1. With feet firmly planted, begin to swing your arms back and forth, like short uppercut punches. The arm and forearm should be at a 90-degree angle. The hand should form a loosely clenched fist.

2. For every complete cycle (a left and a right), inhale once, and for the next cycle exhale, as follows:

$$\frac{\text{left, right}}{\text{i–n–h–a–l–e}} \text{ and } \frac{\text{left, right}}{\text{e–x–h–a–l–e}} \text{ and}$$

$$\frac{\text{left, right}}{\text{i–n–h–a–l–e}} \text{ and } \frac{\text{left, right}}{\text{e–x–h–a–l–e}}.$$ The arms should always remain at a 90-degree angle. Keep the elbows close in, skimming the sides. The fist should come in from the back swing at a slight angle to mid-chest. Continue for 30 seconds. Stomach out while inhaling, in while exhaling.

Basic Cool-down Exercises

Ten Exercises to Stretch and Relax You after Your Workout

These should be done after a workout, but by all means do more if you feel you need special attention for any given area. Taking the time to do these cool-down exercises will not only make you feel better right after your workout, but you will certainly be looser as you begin your next day's training.

HANG LOOSE

After your training, your lower back and hamstrings will feel a bit tight. Here is where you can let gravity do its work.

1. Assume a wide stance. Inhale. Exhale and bend forward, letting your arms, head and body hang. Breathe into the position. Move your upper body easily to the left, back to center, to the right, and back to center. Hold for 20–30 seconds.

2. Stand upright and relax.

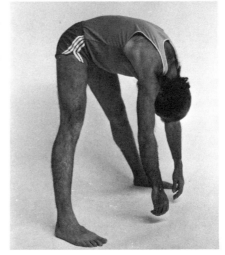

SQUAT STRETCH

This cool-down exercise is exactly the same as the *Prekinetics* warm-up on p. 89.

ACHILLES AND CALF STRETCH

This cool-down exercise is exactly the same as the *Prekinetics* warm-up on p. 77.

HIP STRETCH

This cool-down exercise is exactly the same as the *Prekinetics* warm-up on p. 91.

BACK OVER, KNEES BENT

The purpose of this exercise is to let gravity help to stretch out your back and relax you, without doing the hamstrings.

1. Lie on your back, hands at your sides, feet and toes together. Lift up your head, and look down at your feet to see if your body is in a straight line.

2. Inhale and lift your feet straight up and back behind your head.

3. Bring your knees down by your ears. You can help yourself reach this position by grasping your ankles once your legs are overhead. Keep trying if you find it difficult at first, and you will find you can breathe into the position. Hold for 15–20 seconds.

BEND AND TWIST

This cool-down exercise is exactly the same as the *Prekinetics* warm-up on p. 84.

INVERTED V

This cool-down exercise is exactly the same as the *Prekinetics* warm-up on p. 79.

HEAD ROLLS

This cool-down exercise is exactly the same as the *Prekinetics* warm-up on p. 75.

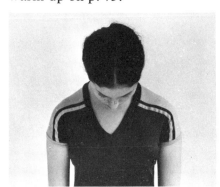 

BABY'S REST

The gentle stretch at the small of the back is like a delicate massage. And now you begin to relax.

1. Remaining on your hands and knees from the previous exercise, sit back on your heels, rest your chest on your thighs and your head on the floor. Reach back and grasp your heels. Try to pull at your heels and push your buttocks downward. You will feel a further stretch of your back.

2. Breathe slowly. Drop your hands to the floor, palms facing upward. Relax for 30–60 seconds.

3. Sit up on your heels, and do the next exercise in that position.

COMPLETE RELAXATION

Please give yourself 10 minutes for this position. You'll be amazed at its restorative benefits.

1. Lie on your back with your arms and legs apart from your body, palms facing up. Place your head so that the back of your neck feels as if it's on the floor. Close your eyes. Breathe deeply, slowly.

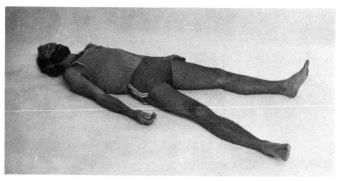

2. Lift up your feet about 6 inches from the floor and tighten every muscle in your feet and legs. Squeeze harder! Now drop them to the floor as if someone were holding them and dropped them. Relax.

3. Tighten your fists and arms, raising them 6 inches from the floor. Squeeze harder! Drop them! Relax.

4. Tighten your buttocks and anus muscles. Squeeze! Relax.

5. Tighten up your face like a prune. Squeeze! Relax.

6. Open your mouth and eyes. Try to touch your tongue to your chin and try to look up over your eyebrows. Relax.

7. Inhale, filling up only your stomach, and hold your breath. Hold it longer—longer. Open your mouth and let the air rush out.

8. Inhale, filling up your chest only. Take in a little more and a little more. Now open your mouth and let the air gush out. Relax and remain motionless. Breathe deeply, slowly.

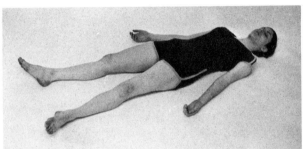

9. Think only of relaxation. Let it start at the bottom of your feet, like a gentle caress. Let thoughts of relaxation spread to your toes, your feet, your legs. Let your knees sink to the floor. Relax every muscle. Relax your skin. Relax your thighs, buttocks, anus, the small of your back, your arms, top and bottom, hands, fingers. Relax your shoulders, neck, chin, face, eyes, ears, scalp. Relax your whole being. Think of nothing. Just allow thoughts to come into your head one at a time. Drift. Relax.

10. After a few minutes, bring your awareness back to your breathing. Breathe more deeply. Curl your toes. Rotate your ankles. Wiggle your fingers. Stretch your arms overhead. Open your eyes and sit up.

You are ready to tackle the world!

KEEPING SCORE
The Pulse Rate Method

As was stated earlier, working the heart will cause it to pump faster, adapt to the work load, and become more efficient. Raising the heart rate is absolutely essential to enhance cardiovascular fitness. When the heart works harder, it helps raise the pulse rate to what is called the training effect or target zone. Once the pulse rate reaches that zone, the training effects or benefits really begin. So in order to get benefit from an exercise program, you should reach that target zone and maintain the effort for a period of time—30 minutes of continuous exercise at that rapid pulse rate at least three times a week is generally considered to be ideal for continuing fitness.

Several clinical studies have been made to determine just how high a human being's heart rate can go. Physiologists have determined that the maximum number of heartbeats is that of a young child: 220 beats per minute. It has also been determined that as you grow older, your maximum heart rate drops about a beat a year. Therefore, if you are 20 years of age, you would subtract 20 from the established maximum of 220, leaving 200. A 30-year-old would have a maximum heart rate of 190, a 40-year-old a maximum heart rate of 180, and so on.

The target heart rate range is determined by taking 70–85 percent of your maximum heart rate. That is the most desirable range for you, at your age, to achieve during training. The chart shows the heart rate best for your age group.

AGE	TARGET HEART RATE
10–19	145 to 180 beats per minute
20–29	140 to 170 beats per minute
30–39	130 to 160 beats per minute
40–49	125 to 150 beats per minute
50–59	115 to 140 beats per minute
60–69	105 to 130 beats per minute
70–79	100 to 120 beats per minute

Pulse rates are easily determined. After walking briskly for 10 minutes, stop and immediately count your pulse by placing your 2nd, 3rd and 4th fingers along the thumb side of your inner wrist, or by placing those same three fingers on your temple. Count the beats for 10 seconds on your watch, then multiply that number by 6. For example, during that 10 seconds you counted 25, multiplied by 6 = 150. You are 33 years of age . . . about 80 percent of your maximum.

The pulse rate method determines where you are in terms of effort. It will help you reach your target zone so that you can get maximum benefit from the exercise. If you find that you were really moving along and you didn't even reach your target zone, then you might want to increase your pace and push a bit harder into the workout. But don't be a slave to pulse counting. Walk the way you feel. Take your pulse once during your workout, preferably at the midpoint. There are those who will take it religiously, and there are those who will forget or not want to break their rhythm. I find it a good tool to use once in a while. I don't always like to keep score.

THE TECHNIQUE OF RACEWALKING

Walk, just walk. O.K. So that's an oversimplification. But seriously, racewalking for fitness can be just that easy. Don't let the word racewalking scare you. At your level, it is nothing more than brisk walking with more attention paid to your arm action than ever before in your conscious thoughts. I say conscious because many of you have racewalked without realizing it. How about the times you were running at the swimming pool to get another turn at the diving board when the lifeguard cautioned, "No running." So you and the other children walked as fast as your little legs could carry you to the board. Or the times when you were hurrying to the movie and couldn't run anymore. You speeded up your normal "streetwalking" action and automatically bent your arms to help your rhythm and balance. Do you remember now?

Most people think that the movements involved in walking appear to be relatively simple. Actually, analysis has shown them to be exceedingly complex. The synchronization of muscular action and joint movements beautifully illustrates the teamwork present in all bodily movements. The most skilled engineers cannot duplicate, even with the most complex piece of machinery, the movements of the human machine in smoothness of function or in perfection of detail. We have the machinery to work with, so let's put it to work.

I'm sure you have heard or used the word: gait. Gait—according to Webster—is a manner of walking. An understanding of gait and the gait cycle will help you tune in better on your body during your training and help you to smooth out your style. No two people the world over will walk the same. They will employ the same technique but develop different styles due to the differences in body types and energies employed. Each walker's gait should be perfected for maximum efficiency.

The Gait Cycle is the time of the contact of the heel of one foot, going to the contact of the heel of the other foot, and back to the original foot, thereby involving two steps. During this period, we have two times when both feet are on the ground at the same time.

These are called the double-limb-support period (above)—that is, when the heel of the right foot and the toe of the left foot are on the ground, and vice versa. We also have two periods when only one foot is on the ground.

The double-limb-support period.

The other foot is swinging freely through the air (below). At no time in walking are both feet off the ground, whereas in running, both feet can be off the ground at the same time. In walking, when a foot contacts the ground, it begins the support or stance phase. When it leaves the ground after pushing off, it begins the swing phase.

The left heel has just planted, and the right foot is just about to swing forward.

As a rule we spend more time on the ground than in the air. The stance phase from point of contact to the actual push-off accounts for 60 percent of that leg's gait action and the swing phase for 40 percent. Most injuries occur during this phase, primarily due to faulty mechanics. Normal pronation (flattening of the foot) begins at contact and ends well into mid-stance. Under normal circumstances the foot must adapt to the ground immediately upon contact. A normal amount of pronation gives forward mobility. Reaching mid-stance the foot begins to supinate (joints become rigid) and prepares for propulsion (push-off). Excessive pronation, if it begins too early, moves too deep or remains too long, keeps the foot in a flexible position, causing undue stress on bones, tendons and ligaments. You must have rigid levers to transport your weight. You will learn how to stabilize your foot, ankle and leg so as to produce a rigid lever at the proper moment in your gait. With that rigidity, you will accomplish the kinetic alignment necessary for trouble-free walking. All your weight rests on your foot. If it isn't strong and properly placed, your whole body can be out of alignment.

Walking is an automatic action; once the initial step is taken, no further conscious control is necessary. Racewalking, with attention to certain refinements of technique, can be reflexive in nature, allowing you to enjoy all that you see, hear and smell around you as you take your workout.

Walking has been described as an alternating loss and recovery of balance. This being so, a new base of support must be established with every step. An illustration of this can be understood very easily. Stand erect with both feet together, arms at your sides. Lean forward from your ankles. As you continue to lean forward, there will be a point where you will begin to fall toward the ground. Instinctively, you will extend your leg (lever) in order to prevent your falling down. If you now swing your other leg (lever) forward, you will be walking.

Of course, in racewalking we attempt to develop as smooth a gait as possible by focusing on optimum mechanical efficiency with our arms and legs. We look to eliminate superfluous up-and-down and side-to-side movements, concentrating more on forward fluidity.

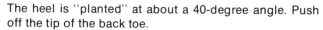

The heel is "planted" at about a 40-degree angle. Push off the tip of the back toe.

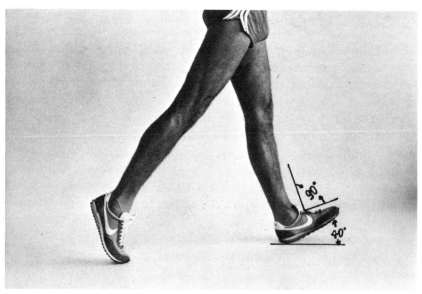

It is most important to feel and analyze what you are doing so that you master the refinements of racewalking. Walk slowly in the beginning, tuning in on your body and feeling how the muscles are performing each segmented action. By committing them to each action again and again, taking care that you are doing them right, you will "groove" your muscles just as a tennis player "grooves" his forehand or a golfer, her swing. Then your walking and your racewalking will be reflexive and fluid.

Again, standing erect with your arms at your sides, begin to walk forward starting with your left foot. With your toes pointing in the direction of your walk, reach out with your hip, your knee and your heel so that you "plant" your heel at about a 40-degree angle. Notice that the foot and leg are at a 90-degree angle. Make sure that the back edge of the heel strikes first.

Here is an exercise to help you get the feeling of coming down on the back edge of your heel. Simply walk a few yards on your heels only.

This is the moment of contact—the point at which you can save yourself from runners knee and many other aches and pains. As the edge of your heel strikes, *tilt* your foot only slightly to the outside edge of your shoe (only enough to get a thin pencil or a fingertip under the inside edge), and "set" (lock) your ankle. The outside edge of your shoes will become rockers, allowing a smooth transition from heel to big toe. By locking your ankle you will be preventing the

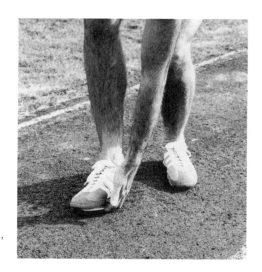

This is accomplished by "setting" the ankle slightly to the outside.

ankle from dropping to the inside and avoiding the excessive internal rotation of the leg which causes chondromalacia patella (runners knee).

As you are pulling forward with the left leg, you should be pushing straight back with the right leg until toe-off. This powerful thrust straight back with the rear leg gives you forward acceleration. Each leg performs two separate actions. One action is to pull the body forward over the leg. Once the body is over that leg, the other action is that same leg pushing the body forward. The only time that leg is not pulling or pushing is when it is in the swing phase of reaching forward after push-off to become the supporting leg again.

Now we will begin to make efficient use of the arms. As you continue walking you will notice that you have been swinging your arms rhythmically, each arm swinging forward with the opposite leg. Bend your arms so that you make a right angle between your upper arm and your forearm. The reason for the right angle is actually to shorten your arm. If you walked with straightened arms, it would be like trying to swing a long pendulum. Your legs might be able to move faster, but because the leg and arm swings are coordinated, the long pendulum (long arm) would tend to slow down your leg speed. By bending the arm at the elbow, you create a shorter pendulum (measured now shoulder to elbow) which can move faster. Now you can make short pistonlike strokes with your arms, synchronized with the quick steps of your legs.

With the elbows close in, just skimming the body, imagine that a nail is in your shoulder holding that right-angled arm, and that the arm is swinging on that nail. Again, skim the body. If your elbows are held too far out from your body like "wings," the tops of your arms from the shoulder to the elbow will tire. Just let your arms hang loosely at your sides and then bend your arm at the elbow. You will still feel the inside of your upper arm skimming your body.

Your swinging arms will help you maintain good balance and forward thrust. You will get a feeling of power as you swing your loosely clenched fists almost like uppercut punches. Your fists should reach their high point at mid-chest (the breastplate). On the backswing, if you are really moving fast, the elbow, upper arm and the shoulder will be almost in a straight line. At slower speeds your arms will not be so high in back or in front. The angle of the swing should be from just skimming the body to just about mid-chest.

Some thoughts about posture: If you learn to racewalk properly, you will improve your posture. In the beginning it will require a lot of attention to put together good racewalking technique, but after a while, as I said earlier, it will become reflexive. Your attention may be directed elsewhere, such as the terrain, the scenery, your conversation, but there should always be a part of your thinking concerned with your technique.

Posture is a gauge of mechanical efficiency, of muscle balance and of neuromuscular coordination. Your attention to technique will help you to achieve the efficiency, balance and coordination that will reflect in good posture.

It is important to walk tall—to "grow" from the back of the neck and achieve a high center of gravity, which is necessary for full leg extension and a resultant longer stride. The feeling from within is like stretching your spine from your tailbone up to your head. Keep your back straight. The straight spine will also help your breathing by keeping your chest cavity opened. Keep your head square on your shoulders, your neck relaxed. If your head is carried too far back or

too far forward, it will cause strain and tension in your neck. Find that comfortable spot for you. Don't tilt your head down to see where you are going. Instead, focus your eyes on a spot 4–5 yards in front of you. Don't worry. You will be able to see the stones, potholes, puddles, etc.

The photo shows an erect carriage with the head squared on the shoulders, eyes focused ahead. Notice that the arms are just about at the high point of their swing. The left fist has crossed the body slightly to mid-chest. The right shoulder, arm and elbow are almost horizontal.

Don't look down to see if you are walking correctly. Instead, feel it from within. Concentrate on the muscular actions involved, and *will* your body to walk. It is good to find a training partner so that you can correct each other's form. Sometimes another person will spot something wrong that you just didn't feel you were doing. And when you or both of you are in doubt, come back to the book and go through that phase again.

After a while you will be focusing only on the weak points in your technique until they too will smooth out. Then you will walk fluidly, correctly, efficiently. After all, that is your purpose: to make yourself an efficient walking machine so that you can enjoy all the benefits of this great exercise. And don't be concerned with speed. Developing good technique is the most important consideration.

I hope you didn't hold your breath through all of this technique business. But seriously, correct breathing during your training is vital. Just as the proper mixture of air and fuel go through the carburetor of your car, that is how your body needs the proper concentration of oxygen carried along by the blood to reach all the cells in your body. Diaphragmatic or belly breathing is the most efficient way to supply your system with all that needed oxygen. I hope you practiced your cadence breathing in the *Prekinetics* warm-up because now you are going to need it. Remember swinging your arms to a count? If the arms and legs are well synchronized, your breathing can be blended right in with them and regulated according to your speed, your steps and your needs at the time. If remembering all the points of technique and now adding regulated breathing seems difficult to you, don't worry. As I have said before, much of your racewalking will be reflexive. It is only in the beginning that you have to think about what you are doing. But that thinking is good because it tunes you into your body. So hang in there for a while and don't become discouraged if you can't put it all together right away. It will come— and faster than you think.

Back to breathing. Try this: Pace around the room. As you extend your left leg, inhale through your nose, pushing your stomach out. Now as you extend your right leg, blow the air out of your mouth and tighten your rib cage and stomach muscles—left leg inhale—right leg exhale—left leg inhale—right leg exhale. Not *after* you take the step! *As* you take the step.

$$\frac{\text{left leg}}{\text{inhale}} \text{ and } \frac{\text{right leg}}{\text{exhale}} \text{ and } \frac{\text{left leg}}{\text{inhale}} \text{ and } \frac{\text{right leg}}{\text{exhale}}$$

You are now on a 2-count cadence. Again:

$$\frac{\text{left leg–(1)}}{\text{i–n–h–a–l–e}} \text{ and } \frac{\text{right leg–(2)}}{\text{e–x–h–a–l–e}} \text{ and } \frac{\text{left leg–(1)}}{\text{i–n–h–a–l–e}} \text{ and } \frac{\text{right leg–(2)}}{\text{e–x–h–a–l–e}}$$

Now let's try a 4-count cadence.

$$\frac{\text{left leg, right leg}}{\text{i--n--h--a--l--e}} \text{ and } \frac{\text{left leg, right leg}}{\text{e--x--h--a--l--e}} \text{ and}$$

$$\frac{\text{left leg (1) right leg (2)}}{\text{i--n--h--a--l--e}} \text{ and } \frac{\text{left leg (3) right leg (4)}}{\text{e--x--h--a--l--e}}$$

You don't have to count out loud. Just think 1–2 or 1, 2–3, 4; and move your legs and breathe in that rhythm.

When would you use each cadence? According to your pace (speed). If you were just cruising along at 15-minute miles, you might be comfortable with the 4 count which is slower. But if you were to increase your pace to 13 or even 12 minutes per mile you might need the 2 count. Just be sure to take full breaths. Use your stomach and ribs like a bellows, forcing the waste air out of your system.

Now let's consider inhaling through your nose as opposed to your mouth. As has been explained before, nasal inhalation cleanses the air more than mouth inhalation. But cold weather may "pinch" your nostrils, or allergies or a cold or a deviated septum may prevent nasal inhalation. Well, we can't leave you gasping for breath. By all means open your mouth and breathe. Also, if your pace is quick and you feel that you are not getting enough air, open your mouth and suck in as much as you can.

So now go out and practice (after your warm-up) and work on your technique, focusing on one thing at a time. First, concentrate on reaching out with your hip, your knee and your heel. Body erect, head up, swing your arms. Get those elbows in closer to your sides. Loosen your fists. Don't clench them. Here's how to do it, step by step.

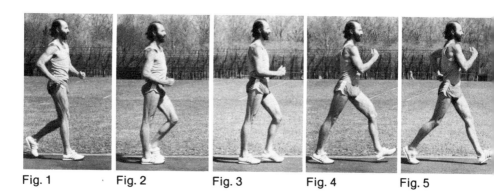

Fig. 1   Fig. 2   Fig. 3   Fig. 4   Fig. 5

Fig. 1: The body is in good balance, with the right leg supporting the body and bracing against the ground while pulling the trunk forward. (Note contracting muscles at front of thigh.) Left leg has begun its forward swing.

Fig. 2: The body and right leg are in a vertical position, with the left leg moving forward, the foot close to the ground. The arms are at the low point of their swing.

Fig. 3: The right leg is hyperextended and its strong push propels the body forward, resulting in a slight forward lean of the trunk. The left leg is reaching out with the foot low to the ground.

Fig. 4: The right leg is exerting its strong thrust to push the body forward. The left leg is reaching out. (Note muscles on inside of thigh extending it forward.) The left lower leg and foot are relaxed.

Fig. 5: The right leg is pushing forward vigorously. (Note the bending of the foot onto the toe.) The left leg has almost straightened. The heel is ready to plant. The arms have almost reached the high point of their swing while the right shoulder has rotated forward slightly to compensate for the extension of the left hip, thereby maintaining good forward balance.

Fig. 6: The heel of the left foot has just made contact, and the foot is beginning its roll forward to the toe (remember this is accomplished slightly on the outside of the foot).

Fig. 7   Fig. 8   Fig. 9   Fig. 10   Fig. 11

The left thigh (quadriceps group) muscles are contracting and pulling the body forward. The right foot has just accomplished the toe-off and is starting its swing forward. Note the arms at approximately a right angle.

Fig. 7: The left foot is rolling forward toward the toe with the quadriceps pulling vigorously. Note that the stripes on the shorts are in a vertical line with the body.

Fig. 8: As in Figure 2 the supporting leg and body are in a vertical position. The arms are at the low point of their swing.

Fig. 9: The left heel is rising as the push forward has begun from the toe to the buttocks. Look at the top of the right leg. The quadriceps group are extend-

ing the leg up and forward. The right foot is relaxed and preparing to plant the heel.

Fig. 10: This is almost at the split-second, double-support phase, where both feet are on the ground at the same time. The right heel is reaching out, about to plant. Note the position of the stripes on the shorts. The right hip has reached forward well in front of the vertical axis of the body. Note that the left leg has driven forward all the way onto the toe. The arms are at a 90-degree angle and at the high point of their swing.

Fig. 11: The right heel has planted. The right thigh muscles are pulling as in Figure 1, and the whole cycle begins again.

I hope that you enjoyed your first workout because now you are going to learn some more refinements of racewalking technique.

Sir Isaac Newton, who lived from 1642 to 1727, was the English physicist who developed the Newtonian Laws of Motion. I think that if he were living now and were a track coach, he would be a mighty good one. Applying his theories of physics especially for runners and racewalkers will produce faster and more injury-free performances. More coaches today should focus their attentions to the technical aspects of running and racewalking.

The Newtonian Law of Reaction: *For every action there is an equal and opposite reaction.* For example, when a person walks across a floor, the feet push back against the floor with the same amount of force as the floor pushes forward against the feet. Therefore, it is important to maximize the thrust forward at the propulsive stage of the foot stance. Keeping this in mind, we must also understand the Newtonian Law of Acceleration: *Acceleration of an object is directly proportional to the force causing it and is in the same direction as the force.* This means that the floor pushing back against the foot is pushing it and the leg and the body forward (same direction) with the same force that the foot exerted against the floor in the first place. So, in order to maximize the thrust forward, which obviously can only be done at push-off, the direction of the foot placement should be such that will allow the toes to push straight back. When the swing leg is reaching out with the hip pushed forward and the knee and the heel reaching out, the toes should be pointed straight ahead so that when heel contact is made, the foot will roll across the outside edge, onto the ball and toes for a straight back push-off. The acceleration can thus be concentrated to the maximum in a straight-ahead direction.

There are some people who walk in a ducklike fashion. We call them out-toers. These people usually pronate (foot rotates outward) excessively. Now that is bad in and of itself, considering the injury rate for overpronators, but in addition, the energy of their push-off is at an angle to the direction of the walk so that maximum forward propulsion is not completely achieved. Some of the force is diffused off to the side, thereby wasting energy. In addition, .8 to 1.0 inches can be lost on each stride. This can be equated to approximately a 220 yard (1 minute) loss over 6 miles or a 440 yard (2 minute) loss over 12 miles. To a competitive racewalker, this can be extremely important. To the average fitness buff, it certainly is important to know when you are doing anything incorrectly in order to be able to correct it and receive maximum benefit and avoid injury.

The following illustration shows proper and improper foot placement:

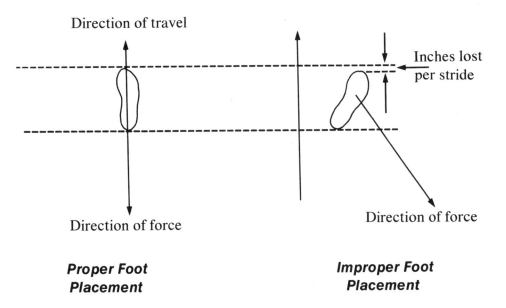

Direction of travel

Inches lost per stride

Direction of force

Direction of force

Proper Foot Placement

Improper Foot Placement

We have just examined how one foot should be placed. But how about one foot compared to the other? For competitive racewalkers, I will go over this in detail in the chapter on competitive racewalking beginning on page 159. The following study of foot placement in relation to gait width is for beginner and recreational racewalkers.

Gait width is the lateral distance between the limbs upon foot placement during a complete stride (two steps). If you have ever noticed the way some fat people walk with their feet far apart, it is because their fat thighs are in the way. Their stride is short and they sway from side to side. At the speeds at which you will be moving, I believe in having the feet no more than 2 inches apart. This can best be illustrated as follows:

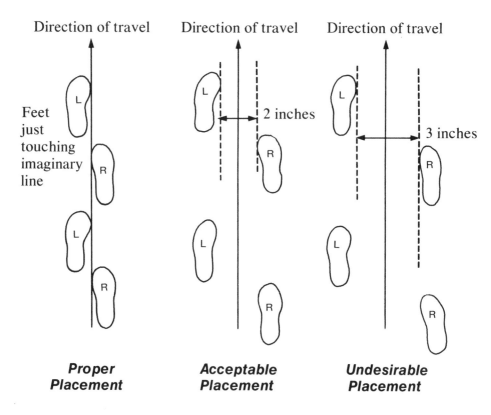

Direction of travel   Direction of travel   Direction of travel

Feet just touching imaginary line

2 inches

3 inches

Proper Placement   ***Acceptable Placement***   ***Undesirable Placement***

Any distance 3 inches or more will tend to produce both an unde-sirable side-to-side sway (restricting forward fluidity) and a shorter stride.

Experiment with the other two placements and determine for your-self what is comfortable for you. If your thighs are on the heavy side now, your gait width will be a bit wider than it will be as your thighs become slimmer. The wider child-bearing pelvis of the female may also feel more comfortable with the slightly wider gait width.

At this point, you have all the components necessary for putting together a smooth, efficient style. The movements that I have de-scribed to you in detail are neither complicated nor hard to do. There are no movements which you cannot do as is proved by the very fact that you all walk already. We're just refining your movements to best advantage.

I'm looking out the window now at a young woman passing by, seemingly in a hurry. With quick steps, her left arm carrying a brief-case, her right arm swinging briskly, she really is moving rapidly. At a slightly faster pace, with 90-degree arm action, she could be race-walking!

With attention to the coaching instructions and tuning in on your body, you will be able to add the refinements of racewalking, which will develop your muscles, build your cardiovascular fitness (the most important fitness of all) and turn you on to two of the most enjoyable pleasures of life: your body and your exercise. Racewalking will do it!

Drive straight back with the rear leg!

Eli Attar

PROFILE OF A CHAMPION
Larry Young

During the entire history of the Olympic Games, only five medals have ever been won by American racewalkers. Larry Young has won two of them. At Mexico City in 1968, Larry placed 3rd in the 50 kilometers racewalk, winning the Bronze Medal. In Munich, in 1972, Larry did it again.

Larry Young was born on February 10, 1943, in Independence, Missouri, the hometown of that other famous walker, President Truman. As a high school runner, he ran respectable times of 2:10 for the half-mile and 4:38 for the mile. He was fascinated with racewalking after seeing a television shot of Britain's Don Thompson winning the 50 kilometer racewalk in the 1960 Olympics. After 4 years in the U.S. Navy, he began racewalking in 1965 in some of the All-Comers meets in California. Larry moved up to international class rather quickly. His formula for success stresses technique above all else. "You must concentrate on technique especially during training; otherwise, you won't have it for the race." Larry believes in quality workouts of 85–100 miles per week. Especially when feeling good, his favorite workout is a 10–15 mile push effort, in which he goes all out as if it were a race. Larry also enjoys 5–7 mile Fartlek training and one long workout, 30–35 miles, per week. "You must put in the time on your feet to make it in the 50."

Larry is a sculptor and is currently living in Columbia, Missouri.

"Oh look, dear, that's that funny sport where they all wiggle their behinds while trying to walk fast."

The starter's gun had gone off, and twelve men were engaged in a racewalk on the 11-lap-to-the-mile board track at the old Madison Square Garden. A ripple of laughter and giggling arose from the crowd, but the thick-skinned walkers ignored it all. Henry Laskau, as usual, had taken over the pace and was increasing his lead until he began overtaking the other walkers. Suddenly, instead of snickers and giggles, there arose cheers and shouting, spurring him on. When he broke the tape, there was applause and whistling.

Racewalking is sometimes considered odd because it is out of the ordinary. I mean, if you want to go fast, why not run, right? Wrong. Some people want to run fast and some people want to walk fast. It's as simple as that.

In the early days of jogging many runners had endured sneers and catcalls during training. Racewalkers are just different, that's all.

Admittedly, some walkers affect too much of a side-to-side sway when they racewalk, rather than reaching forward with the hip in order to achieve forward fluidity. A good walker is beautiful to watch —all grace and power, but we walkers have not lost our ability to laugh at ourselves. Because we are enjoying what we are doing for our bodies and our minds, people can laugh all they want at wiggling behinds. Real athletes never laugh at us at all. They appreciate what it takes to be good at our sport. The laughter comes from the smoking, drinking, fat slobs who don't do any exercise. They have the problems, not us.

10

THE COACH'S RACEWALK PROGRAMS
For Beginners: Twelve Weeks of Intensive Care

Just remember that you have been inactive for some time, so you are going to take it nice and easy. I suggest that for the first 2 months you adhere pretty closely to the guidelines set forth in this plan. They will ease you into the program, help you to learn the discipline of the athlete, and prevent you from doing too much too soon. In the beginning, try to stick to the every-other-day routine so that your workouts will be spread over a full week. Your body will adapt better if you allow a day of recuperation after a day of exercise. As little exercise as you might do in the beginning, your body will still need that rest. You might want to take one or both days off on the weekend. That is certainly up to you. Your condition won't be hurt by training only on weekdays. Just make sure you get at least 3–4 training days each week and schedule them so you get a recuperative day in between.

Some of you are in fairly good shape even now, at the start of this program. I don't want you, especially during the first 4 weeks, to get carried away and go faster. There is always a faster pace at which you can train for the suggested workout but don't do it. After the first 4 weeks, you may train at a faster pace and if you find even that exceedingly slow for you, train at a minute faster per mile for 2 weeks. Then see where you are. If you want to go still faster, train at another minute faster per mile. But don't step things up any way except gradually.

Now we are rapidly approaching that time when push comes to shove. The time that you make the commitment to yourself as to

122

when you are actually going to begin the program. Pick a target date for beginning, the first day of the month or whatever day is convenient for you to start. I record my training from Sunday through Saturday, coordinating with most calendars. Set the date. Survey the site on which you will train. Make sure that it is well lighted at the hour when you will train. If it's on a road, see if the road slopes to the outside. If you walk facing traffic, your right foot will take undue pressure from the slope. It would be better to try and find an alternate route. Have all your gear in readiness well before. Set it on a chair or a shelf so that you will see it often. Tell a couple of friends that you are going to start or arrange to start with a friend or two. If you are overweight, begin restricting your caloric intake a few days beforehand, as if you were preparing for a big event. The chapter entitled "Looking Athletic" begins on page 199. You must prepare yourself mentally for this "happening." You must be disciplined. If a friend "cops out," keep *your* resolve. It's *your* body and it's *your* life, so you have to do it all alone if need be.

Most working people prefer the early morning workout because it "sets them up" for their day. They arrive at work awake, fresh and ready. It also assures that a busy social life or a night course or a late meeting doesn't interfere with their training schedule. Morning people seem to adhere to their training schedules better than after-work people. Many housewives must get the family up and on their way before they can have time for themselves. As long as you haven't eaten with the family (sure, a cup of coffee or tea is O.K.), you can train right after they leave. It can be pretty quiet at those hours, so just be sure that any secluded areas you choose are safe. Better to walk around your block a few times than to stroll too lonely a wooded path. Better safe than sorry. Those of you who can arrange to train during your lunch hour (or two?), you've got a darned good deal. Enjoy!

There are those who just can't seem to pop out of bed and start training right away. Suit yourself. But be prepared to have things come up that may conflict with the appointed hour for your training. Be strong, but be flexible. Don't turn down too many invitations nor lose out on that night course in the foreign language that you always wanted to learn. Life is too short. I believe in discipline when one really wants to accomplish something but not at the expense of an enjoyable life. When you begin to enjoy and look forward to your workouts, you will arrange the rest of your schedule to fit them in. If you enjoy reading or bowling with friends, you can fit them in also. If you give up too many things just for your training, you are going to resent it, or your wife or husband or boy- or girlfriend will. Enjoy it all—just find a good balance.

You've set the day; now set the hour. Arrange to get a good night's sleep the night before. If you are not used to getting up so early, put the alarm clock or radio across the room so that you have to get out of bed to shut it off. *Don't* get back into bed. Get going.

If your wife or husband or friend or lover or whoever shares your room still sleeps, take your gear into another room before you do your exercises. Do your warm-up stretching slowly and fully. Don't take any shortcuts. Visit the bathroom once more and finish dressing. Don't forget to bring toilet paper with you. Some people's bowels are more sluggish in the first hours of the morning, but then they suddenly awake during a workout. Keep your eyes open for "pit stops" —bushes, trees, buildings that provide cover.

Slowly and easily. This is a break-in period, remember? I don't want any racing, any pushing, any overdoing. For these first few weeks you are going to do the complete warm-up and cool-down exercise routines and easy racewalking. I want you to train so that you are pleasantly tired. Not wiped out or exhausted. Some of you may have no discomfort whatsoever, but in the beginning, you may experience some minor aches and pains. You will be using muscles that you haven't used in many years. With regular training, the discomfort will go away. Accept some minor crying out from your muscles. You neglected them for so long, and now they are saying, "It's your fault that you didn't work us before, but now you had better keep it up so that we can get stronger and don't have this soreness."

For the first 4 weeks, walk at 90–120 steps per minute which will give you about 15–20 minutes per mile. You don't have to count all the time. After a while there will be no need because you will feel the pace. In the beginning there is a lot to do and to remember, but don't worry, you will be able to put it together with little difficulty.

Now, go out and train.

The Coach's Racewalk Programs: For Beginners

WEEK 1

Don't forget your Prekinetics *warm-up before each workout.*

WORKOUT	COACH'S COMMENTS
SUNDAY	
20-min. racewalk at 90-120 steps per minute	Focus on arm and leg rhythm
MONDAY	
Rest	
TUESDAY	
20-min. racewalk at 90-120 steps per minute	Focus on foot placement
WEDNESDAY	
Rest	
THURSDAY	
20-min. racewalk at 90-120 steps per minute	Focus on arm and leg rhythm
FRIDAY	
Rest	
SATURDAY	
Prekinetics warm-up only	*Got to keep limber*

Don't forget your cool-down exercises.

Take your pulse before you start and again when you are 10 minutes into a workout. If you are in your training range, continue as you are. Don't worry this week if you have not reached your training range. I would rather that you get your body accustomed to the work first. If you can't handle the pace, slow down until you can handle it comfortably. If you feel really tired, do only 8 to 10 minutes or whatever you can. Tomorrow is another day.

If your muscles feel sore or tight, take a hot bath at night. Everyone may feel some soreness on the front of the lower leg, toward the outside. This comes from flexing your foot to accommodate your heel plant. It will go away with work. Buy some baby oil or skin lotion and give yourself a massage. Have someone give you a foot massage, or give yourself one. There is nothing like it.

WEEK 2

Don't forget your Prekinetics *warm-up before each workout.*

WORKOUT	COACH'S COMMENTS
SUNDAY	
20-min. racewalk at 90-120 steps per minute	Focus on an upright posture
MONDAY	
Rest	
TUESDAY	
20-min. racewalk at 90-120 steps per minute	Focus on arm and leg rhythm
WEDNESDAY	
Prekinetics warm-up only	*Stay loose*
THURSDAY	
20-min. racewalk at 90-120 steps per minute	Focus on foot placement, straight back push
FRIDAY	
Rest	
SATURDAY	
20-min. racewalk at 100-120 steps per minute	Keep your head up, not *back*, just up

Don't forget your cool-down exercises.

PROFILE OF A CHAMPION
Dave Romansky

Incredibly strong . . . that's Dave Romansky, born April 8, 1938. Dave is 6 feet 2 inches and constantly has a weight problem. His weight varies from close to 200 pounds to 163 pounds when he is in top shape. Romansky is a former mediocre road runner turned international class racewalker in a brief 2 years. He started racewalking in 1967 and immediately found himself with style problems. He and I went over basic techniques and straightened out the problems for some of his longer racing. Dave's amazing strength has gotten him through some super races, but at times he would "pull" himself off the ground with his arms. He has since eliminated that problem. In 1968 he won his first national championship, at the 40 kilometer in Long Branch, New Jersey, and made the 50 kilometer team for the Olympics in Mexico City after only a year and a half of racewalking.

In 1970 he had a great year, setting American records at distances from 1,500 meters to 10,000 meters. His trip to Europe was successful. He beat the Germans and the French and lost to the Russians, but he posted a record 1:29:50 for the 20km. On a trip to Sweden in 1978 Dave, already turned 40, walked an incredible 20 kilometers in 1:33. When he makes up his mind to work, he works! Some of Dave's startling workouts are described on page 187.

The two Romansky daughters, Denise age 15, and Diana age 9, coached by their father, have been walking for a couple of years now and have set various age group records. The Romansky family resides in Pennsville, New Jersey. Dave has worked for the Du Pont Corporation for many years.

If you have done your stretching faithfully and you haven't pushed faster than the recommended pace, you shouldn't be muscle sore or tired. In fact, you should be feeling pretty good about yourself. If during your workouts, you will focus on one element of your technique during that session, you will find yourself improving as you go along. Even though walking is reflexive, racewalking will be a new learning experience for you. In the beginning, many people exhibit a rather contrived arm motion while trying to coordinate the arms and legs together. If your arms don't feel right, keep walking at the same speed while letting your arms hang loosely at your sides. They will start to swing with the opposite leg. When they do, simply bend them to that 90-degree angle and continue that rhythm. From the shoulder to the elbow, the arm swings the same whether straight or bent. Concentrate on your foot placement, landing on the heel, locking the ankle slightly to the outside, and rolling along the foot to push off. Are you checking your pulse rate? For those of you who can walk faster . . . don't!

By now you should feel more comfortable with the racewalking technique. But many people still don't make enough use of their arms. They hold them in a bent position and move their legs, but their arms look as though they are carrying a tray of teacups. *Swing* your arms *vigorously* like an uppercut punch. Let them work for you.

WEEK 3

Do I really have to remind you about warm-up?

WORKOUT	COACH'S COMMENTS
SUNDAY	
20-min. racewalk at 90-120 steps per minute	Elbows in, loosely clenched fist
MONDAY	
Prekinetics warm-up	
TUESDAY	
30-min. racewalk at 90-120 steps per minute	Begin to synchronize your breathing
WEDNESDAY	
Prekinetics warm-up	
THURSDAY	
30-min. racewalk at 90-120 steps per minute	Focus on foot placement, stride width
FRIDAY	
Rest	
SATURDAY	
20-min. racewalk at 100-120 steps per minute	Don't tilt your head to one side

If you miss a workout, combine the Prekinetics *and the cool-down.*

While taking a workout on East End Avenue yesterday morning, I must have encountered six or seven people running in the street in the same direction as traffic. I suggested that they would be safer running facing traffic. They all thanked me and switched to the other side of the street.

WEEK 4

Your warm-up should be like second nature by now.

WORKOUT	COACH'S COMMENTS
SUNDAY	
30-min. racewalk at 90-120 steps per minute	Reach out with hip, knee and heel
MONDAY	
Prekinetics warm-up	
TUESDAY	
30-min. racewalk at 90-120 steps per minute	Feel your heel touch and roll to your toe
WEDNESDAY	
Prekinetics warm-up	
THURSDAY	
30-min. racewalk at 90-120 steps per minute	Focus on arm and leg rhythm
FRIDAY	
Rest	
SATURDAY	
30-min. racewalk at 90-120 steps per minute	Can you put it all together yet?

If you are tense or tight on an off day, try a cool-down session.

We have been together for a month now. You should feel very comfortable with your racewalking style. If you have doubts, review the chapter on technique and get in front of a mirror or walk downtown during the early morning and look at yourself as you pass the store windows. This is one of the good reasons for finding a training partner, even if you train together only occasionally. You can analyze and correct each other's technique. But I really want you to *feel* your way along—to *feel* it from within. You can look in a mirror or someone can place your arm or leg in a position, but you have to *feel* your own muscles *putting* you in that position. Are you checking your pulse?

This may be a time when admittedly you can find training something of a bore. It is, but it will continue to be worth it. Think it over. Do you expect to be entertained all your life? Can you take a pill and instantly become fit? Bull! We both know that it takes work. So what? Think of what you are doing for your body and your mind. Think of the Greek ideal. Sometimes you have to go through the mundane things to get to the really good stuff, your fitness. So stay with it!

Now, let's get to next week's workout. But first, a little introduction to your second 4 weeks of racewalking. During the past month you have been racewalking at a pace of approximately 15–18–20 minutes per mile, covering 1½ to 2 miles for each of your last workouts. By now you should be used to the pace. For some of you that may be as fast and as far as you should go in any workout. If you had to slow down your pace because you couldn't handle it, go through another 4 weeks on the same schedule as the first 4 weeks. If you were chafing at the bit to go faster, here is your chance. *But,* go up in slow stages so that you *don't do too much too soon.* I will never get tired of using that phrase. You have heard it already and will hear it some more.

From this point on you will get your workouts in terms of mileage at a given pace. You can always go slower, but for most of you, at this stage, I *don't* want you going faster. You are just not ready.

WEEK 5

If you feel a tightness in a muscle group, warm up with extra time or repetitions spent on that area.

WORKOUT	COACH'S COMMENTS
SUNDAY	
2-mile racewalk at 14-18 min. pace per mile	Focus on feeling your movements
MONDAY	
Prekinetics warm-up	
TUESDAY	
2-mile racewalk at 14-18 min. pace per mile	Focus on synchronized breathing
WEDNESDAY	
Prekinetics warm-up	
THURSDAY	
2-mile racewalk at 14-18 min. pace per mile	Focus on foot placement, toes straight
FRIDAY	
Rest	
SATURDAY	
2.5-mile racewalk at 16 min. pace per mile	Focus on style all the way, feel it

Concentrate on those tight areas in your cool-down.

When you increase your mileage, you may tire near the end. That is the time when you should concentrate on your style so that you can groove your muscles and not develop bad habits. You can experiment with your stride length; try increasing it just a bit. If you ever want to switch your Saturday and Sunday workouts, please feel free to do so. The program should never be inflexible.

There may be a medical reason, or business pressures, or whatever, that may cause you to interrupt your training for a week or two or maybe more. If that happens start over at Week One, and just keep those workouts when and as often as you can until you can arrange your time for training on a regular basis. Then you can follow week by week.

WEEK 6

I'm sure that you have seen significant improvement in your ability to bend and stretch during your Prekinetics *warm-up.*

WORKOUT	COACH'S COMMENTS
SUNDAY 2-mile racewalk at 14-18 min. pace per mile	Try deep breathing to a 4 or 6 count
MONDAY *Prekinetics* warm-up	
TUESDAY 2.5-mile racewalk at 14-18 min. pace per mile	Focus on foot placement, heel to toe
WEDNESDAY *Prekinetics* warm-up	
THURSDAY 2-mile racewalk at 14-18 min. pace per mile	Focus on head in comfortable position
FRIDAY Rest	
SATURDAY 2.5-mile racewalk at 14-18 min. pace per mile	Focus on vigorous uppercut punches

Your cool-down should be sooo R–E–L–A–X–I–N–G.

Your muscles should begin to feel firmer, and if you have cut down on your caloric intake, your body measurements may begin to change. You may not have lost many pounds, but you can lose inches because of muscles firming up. Hang in there. Don't forget to measure your pulse rate from time to time.

An intelligent athlete should know his or her own body inside and out. He should be constantly "tuned in," so that in achieving proper

WEEK 7

Don't forget to close your eyes during some of your Prekinetics.

WORKOUT	COACH'S COMMENTS
SUNDAY	
2-mile racewalk at 14-18 min. pace per mile	You can pick up slightly at end
MONDAY	
Prekinetics warm-up	
TUESDAY	
2-mile racewalk at 14-18 min. pace per mile	Focus on elbows in, loosely clenched fist
WEDNESDAY	
1-mile racewalk at 13-min. pace per mile	Optional—otherwise, your regular pace
THURSDAY	
2.5-mile racewalk at 16 min. pace per mile	Focus on keeping that pace
FRIDAY	
Rest	
SATURDAY	
3-mile racewalk at 14-18 min. pace per mile	Focus on synchronized breathing

The cool-down is like a gentle massage to the muscles.

alignment, better performances and fewer injuries will result. Joe Paterno, great football coach at Penn State University, says he would rather have scholars who want to play football than football players who want to go to college.

O.K. So you have added another day of training to your week, increased your pace a bit, and also added some mileage. Look back to Weeks One and Two. You should be proud of yourself. If you couldn't handle the optional 13-minute mile that I threw in, concentrate on some more distance before you attempt it again.

A "stitch" or pain in the side while running or walking is caused by a spasm of the diaphragm. It is like a charley horse of the dia-

WEEK 8

Prekinetics *now might be done twice a day to feel really loose.*

WORKOUT	COACH'S COMMENTS
SUNDAY	
2-mile racewalk at 14-17 min. pace	*Pace* measured per mile (2 miles in 28-34 minutes)
MONDAY	
Prekinetics warm-up	
TUESDAY	
2.5-mile racewalk at 14-18 min. pace	Focus on upright posture and head
WEDNESDAY	
1.5-mile racewalk at 14-17 min. pace	Focus on synchronized breathing
THURSDAY	
2-mile racewalk at 16 min. pace	Focus on pushing straight back
FRIDAY	
Rest	
SATURDAY	
3-mile racewalk at 14-18 min. pace	Focus on good all-around rhythm

If you have to miss a workout, combine the Prekinetics *and the cool-down.*

phragm muscle. Many people who have been sedentary are beset by stitches because of the sudden and prolonged use of the diaphragm. This is due to incorrect breathing—not breathing deeply enough into your abdomen. Practice the breathing exercise shown in The Science of Breathing and in *Prekinetics*. When you experience a stitch, expel as much air as you can by going "Hoooooo" or "Haaaaaa" or "Uuuuuuuuh" while contracting the stomach muscles. After you have expelled the maximum, start proper diaphragmatic breathing in a regular pattern as found in cadence breathing on page 92.

If you have stuck to a reasonable diet, I am sure that you have lost 6–12 pounds, depending on how overweight you were in the beginning. If you haven't, don't fool yourself. Have you been really good? You have been burning off a lot of calories so if you haven't lost weight, then you've been cheating. This was the end of another 4-week period and you are doing well, so keep it up.

WEEK 9

Now, we begin to pick up the pace even more.

WORKOUT	COACH'S COMMENTS
SUNDAY	
2-mile racewalk at 13-17 min. pace	Focus on elbows in, loosely clenched fist
MONDAY	
Prekinetics warm-up	
TUESDAY	
2.5-mile racewalk at 13-17 min. pace	Focus on uppercut punches, head up
WEDNESDAY	
2-mile racewalk at 13-17 min. pace	Focus on walking tall, "grow" from tailbone to head
THURSDAY	
2-mile racewalk at 13-17 min. pace	Focus on foot placement—roll on the foot, feel it
FRIDAY	
Rest	

SATURDAY

3-mile racewalk at 13-17 min. pace   Focus on putting it all together

Try a cool-down during lunch hour, if you have a private office.

Now just remember, *you don't have to pick up the pace!* Some of you will be able to, some of you won't, and some of you may not *want* to pick it up. That's all right with me. As a coach I have dealt with a broad spectrum of abilities and competitive desires, but this is not competition. You are here as athletes in training for a physical fitness program where you must always walk "within" yourself. You must not feel spent after a workout. If you do, back off and slow down your pace.

WEEK 10

Don't skip your Prekinetics *warm-up.*

WORKOUT	COACH'S COMMENTS
SUNDAY	
2-mile racewalk at 13-17 min. pace	Focus on foot placement, stride width
MONDAY	
Prekinetics warm-up	
TUESDAY	
2.5-mile racewalk at 13-17 min. pace	Focus on synchronized breathing
WEDNESDAY	
2-mile racewalk at 13-17 min. pace	Focus on foot placement, roll on foot
THURSDAY	
3-mile racewalk at 13-17 min. pace	Focus on trying to lengthen stride
FRIDAY	
Rest	
SATURDAY	
2-mile racewalk at 13-17 min. pace	Focus on putting it all together

Don't forget your cool-down.

Some people get rather bored with the same scenery every day. Investigate some alternative sites for your training. Even if you live in a city, try going in and out of different streets near your neighborhood. Your own attitude toward your workout and what it affords your body and mind is important.

WEEK 11

Training without a warm-up is like trying to learn algebra without arithmetic.

WORKOUT	COACH'S COMMENTS
SUNDAY	
3-mile racewalk at 13-17 min. pace	Focus on foot placement. walk light-footed
MONDAY	
Prekinetics warm-up	
TUESDAY	
3-mile racewalk at 13-17 min. pace	Focus on getting those arms up. vigorously
WEDNESDAY	
1-mile racewalk at 12-15 min. pace (optional)	Focus on quick steps
THURSDAY	
2-mile racewalk at 13-17 min. pace	Focus on putting it all together
FRIDAY	
Rest	
SATURDAY	
2-mile racewalk at 13-16 min. pace	Focus on walking tall

A good cool-down will serve you for today and tomorrow.

On Wednesday I asked you to do 1 mile at a pace faster than you have been used to training. That was a little time trial for you to see where you are. If you are still considerably overweight, or not able to handle that speed, then don't try. Keep to the 13–17 min pace and make it a 2–3 mile workout. But most of you should be able by now to walk something a bit faster than a 15-minute mile. Sometimes we have to do a little speed work to jolt us out of a slower, monotonous training pace. Consider it just an exercise in concentration—of moving the legs faster while still maintaining good form.

WEEK 12

You are almost there! Keep on stretching!

WORKOUT	COACH'S COMMENT
SUNDAY	
2-mile racewalk at 13-17 min. pace	Focus on lengthening your stride
MONDAY	
Prekinetics warm-up	
TUESDAY	
3-mile racewalk at 13-17 min. pace	Focus on foot placement, toes pointing straight
WEDNESDAY	
2-mile racewalk at 12-15 min. pace (optional)	Focus on long strides, synchronized arms
THURSDAY	
2-mile racewalk at 14-18 min. pace	Focus—recuperation day, hold form
FRIDAY	
Rest	
SATURDAY	
4-mile racewalk at 13-17 min. pace	Focus on putting it all together with rhythm

You deserve a nice relaxing cool-down!

Well, you have done it! No one can call you a beginner anymore. You are an athlete in every sense of the word. You have earned your varsity letters: L.A., Lifetime Athlete. Congratulations for getting through the most difficult part of the program. The adjustment in your lifestyle, the discipline, the dedication, the minor aches and pains, the occasional boredom show your courage in sticking with it. If you have adhered to the program with a reasonable degree of regularity and watched your diet, your performance over the last 12 weeks can be evaluated in answering the following questions:

1. If weight was your problem, did you lose any?
2. Do you now have more endurance?
3. Are your muscles firmer, stronger?
4. Do you have more vitality?
5. Did you lower your resting pulse rate?
6. Do you feel like an athlete?
7. Are you beginning to look athletic?
8. Aren't you happier with yourself now?

I have no doubt that all of your answers are yes. Nice going.
There are so many good things ahead of you when you are fit, feel fit, and look fit. Stay with The Programs. What you have achieved in a few short weeks is nothing compared to what lies ahead of you.
Shall we go on?

11

THE COACH'S RACEWALK PROGRAMS
For Lifetime Athletes: Keeping Fit Forever

Just because you have earned your varsity letters doesn't mean that you can sit back and rest on your laurels. Being an L.A. (Lifetime Athlete) means making a commitment—a commitment to your mind and to your body, each serving the other. You can add years to your life and quality to those years by keeping that commitment, day by day and year by year. I look forward to my birthdays, and even if it sounds trite, I'm going to say it anyway: I'm getting older *and* I'm getting better.

We (you and I) have brought you to a level of conditioning where you should be in good enough shape to start pushing your body. The colleges and athletic clubs have a system of grading their distance running and racewalking teams. Usually the first and fastest team is called the "A" team, the second is called the "B" team, and the third is called the "C" team. I am going to group you into teams. However, since I don't feel that anyone should be penalized for being slower, the team groupings will be as follows:

"A" Racewalking Team: Those who want to remain with slower-paced racewalking.

"B" Racewalking Team: Those who want to walk a bit faster but don't have competitive goals.

"C" Racewalking Team: Those who want to improve to the point of competing in racewalks.

Choose the team that suits your present condition and your goals. However, you are not locked in to a team or to the workouts that I will prescribe. You can always walk slower, but if you want to walk faster, you have to do so in stages so that your body can adjust. If you had not been with a faster group during weeks seven through twelve, then you must get that foundation and do the fast workouts for those 6 weeks, then move to the "B" or "C" team and begin at Week Thirteen. In actuality, you then would have to do 18 weeks (the first 12, plus the last 6 at the fast pace) before moving to a faster team—if you were in the slow or middle group during weeks seven through twelve.

During this next 12-week period, each team will be guided according to their previous conditioning and their respective goals. The work load each of you will be asked to handle will be consistent with your team's conditioning as a whole. It will not do you any good as an "A" team member to wake up suddenly one day and decide to do the "C" team workout. You can only do what you can do. You shouldn't do what you are not prepared to do.

Even though you will be training harder and pushing your body more, I will show you how to keep that commitment to yourself by making your workouts fun and interesting.

By now your *Prekinetics* and cool-down should be second nature to you. I see no need to remind you constantly to do them. As responsible athletes, you will.

The "A" and "B" teams will train the same number of days for a while. Gradually, you will see the teams clearly separated according to the work loads.

You will definitely find some of your workouts boring. Stay with them. Try meditating while you work out. Just let thoughts come into your head, one at a time. It can be such a private time for you—a time to be alone with your thoughts. By the time you have reached the 24th week, you will see fantastic changes in yourself. Your body will have gone through many changes as you have adapted to the work loads. But your mind as well will profit from this investment of your time and energy.

The Coach's Racewalk Programs: For Lifetime Athletes

WEEK 13

Remember, this is another buildup period so easy does it.

WORKOUT	COACH'S COMMENTS
SUNDAY	
A *Take the day off*	*You've earned it*
B *Take the day off*	*You've earned it*
C *Take the day off*	*You've earned it*
MONDAY	
A 2-mile RW at 15-17 min. pace	
B 2-mile RW at 13-17 min. pace	Focus on synchronized breathing
C 2-mile RW at 13-16 min. pace	
TUESDAY	
A *Prekinetics* warm-up	
B *Prekinetics* warm-up	
C 2-mile RW at 13-16 min. pace	Focus on erect posture
WEDNESDAY	
A 2-mile RW at 15-17 min. pace	
B 2-mile RW at 13-16 min. pace	Focus on foot placement
C 2-mile RW at 13-16 min. pace	
THURSDAY	
A 2-mile RW at 15-17 min. pace	Focus on vigorous arm movement
B 1.5-mile RW at 13-14 min. pace	Focus on quick steps
C 1.5-mile RW at 13 min. pace	
FRIDAY	
A Rest	
B Rest	
C Options day	Your choice: train 2 miles or rest
SATURDAY	
A 3-mile RW at 15-17 min. pace	
B 4-mile RW at 13-15 min. pace	Focus on putting it all together
C 4-mile RW at 13-15 min. pace	

WEEK 14

Relaxed, stretched muscles will do the job.

WORKOUT	COACH'S COMMENTS
SUNDAY	
A 2-mile RW at 15-16 min. pace	Just a bit faster
B 2-mile RW at 13-16 min. pace	
C 2-mile RW at 13-15 min. pace	Focus on walking tall
MONDAY	
A *Prekinetics* warm-up	
B *Prekinetics* warm-up	
C 2-mile RW at 13-15 min. pace	Focus on lengthening your stride
TUESDAY	
A 2-mile RW at 15-16 min. pace	Focus on heel plant. rolling along the foot
B 2.5-mile RW at 13-16 min. pace	
C 2.5-mile RW at 13-15 min. pace	
WEDNESDAY	
A *Prekinetics* warm-up	
B 2-mile RW at 13-16 min. pace	Focus on synchronized arms and legs
C 2-mile RW at 13-15 min. pace	
THURSDAY	
A 2-mile RW at 15-16 min. pace	
B 2.5-mile RW at 13-16 min. pace	Focus on your breathing
C 2.5-mile RW at 13-15 min. pace	
FRIDAY	
A Rest	
B Rest	
C Rest	
SATURDAY	
A Walk in the country for 1 hour	
B Walk in the country for 1½ hours	At your own pace
C Walk in the country for 1½-2 hours	

On the Saturday walk, take a light knapsack or shoulder bag that you can hang across your back and find a complete change of scenery.

When I was coaching the Long Island Athletic Club, we used to go out for walks of 5 to 8 hours. We took money with us and stopped off at various roadside stores to buy juices, bananas, and oatmeal cookies. (Bananas are easily digestible and they are high in potassium, one of many minerals that you lose in perspiration.) We drank and ate lightly and were on our way again.

I want you to go at your own pace just so you get used to spending that time on your feet. With endurance training, the speed doesn't always matter.

Finding a training partner or a group to train with can really help in the beginning when you need some encouragement and understanding of your commitment. A group with a common bond that moves together at the pace of the slowest member is a good example of enjoyable camaraderie.

After this week the pace for the "B" team will step up considerably. You will be increasing both your mileage and your speed. The "C" team members will also move up to another plateau and increase their work load. For you "C" team members who want to increase your mileage even more but don't have the time in the morning, there are many ways that you can accomplish this. Since I don't want you on double workouts yet (you'll have to wait for the competitive section), you can walk all or part of the way home from work. If safety is not a factor, simply walk home in the evening. If it is not far enough, you can get off a station or two before your regular destination. Many people walk home from the commuter railroad station instead of being picked up at the station. Just think of the many ways that you all can walk instead of ride.

Maybe you should also think about being a little tougher on your children. Refuse to drive them anywhere they could walk, provided the weather isn't too bad. You know that it would be for their own good. Set an example for them. Take them out for long walks. Besides the health factor, it's a wonderful way to promote family togetherness.

WEEK 15

A change of scenery brings renewed vigor for everyday workouts.

WORKOUT	COACH'S COMMENTS
SUNDAY	
A Rest	Extra *Prekinetics* to ease any aches
B 2-mile RW at an easy pace	and pains from yesterday
C 2-mile RW at an easy pace	
MONDAY	
A 2-mile RW at 15-16 min. pace	
B 2.5 mile RW at 13-15 min. pace	Focus on lengthening your stride
C 2.5 mile RW at 13-14 min. pace	
TUESDAY	
A *Prekinetics* warm-up	
B *Prekinetics* warm-up	
C 2-mile RW at 13-14 min. pace	Focus on elbows in, loose fist
WEDNESDAY	
A 1 mile at 14 min. pace (optional)	
B 1.5-mile RW at 13 min. pace	Focus on quick steps
C 2-mile RW at 13 min. pace	
THURSDAY	
A 2-mile RW at 15-16 min. pace	
B 2-mile RW at 13-15 min. pace	Focus on walking tall
C 2-mile RW at 13-14 min. pace	
FRIDAY	
A Rest	
B Rest	
C Rest	
SATURDAY	
A Walk in the country for 1 hour	
B Walk in the country for 1½ hours	At your own pace
C Walk in the country for 1½-2 hours	

After your cool-down is a great time for a quick Saturday nap.

WEEK 16

"A" team: Train so that you feel pleasantly tired, not wiped out.

WORKOUT	COACH'S COMMENTS
SUNDAY	
A Rest	Extra *Prekinetics* for yesterday and today
B 2-mile RW at an easy pace	
C 2-mile RW at an easy pace	
MONDAY	
A 2-mile RW at 15-16 min. pace	
B 2.5-mile RW at 13-15 min. pace	Focus on feeling the rhythm
C 3-mile RW at 12-14 min. pace	
TUESDAY	
A *Prekinetics* warm-up	
B *Prekinetics* warm-up	
C 2-mile RW at 12-14 min pace	Focus on vigorous arm swing
WEDNESDAY	
A 2.5-mile RW at 15-16 min. pace	
B 3-mile RW at 13-15 min. pace	Focus on uppercut punches
C 3.5-mile RW at 12-14 min. pace	
THURSDAY	
A 2-mile RW at 15-16 min. pace	
B 2-mile RW at 13-15 min. pace	Focus on keeping head comfortable
C 2-mile RW at 12-14 min. pace	
FRIDAY	
A Rest	
B Rest	
C Rest	
SATURDAY	
A 3-mile RW at 15-16 min. pace	
B 4-mile RW at 13-15 min. pace	Focus on walking tall
C 4-mile RW at 12-14 min. pace	

Get a good stretch by leaving your heel on the ground while street walking. Push your hip forward and you will feel the stretch in the groin and the top of the thigh. Also push forward onto your toes to make the calves work more.

To add mileage to your program, you might want to walk your dog.

N. Y. Daily News Photo

WEEK 17

If you're really tired from the previous day, do a double Prekinetics *and skip the workout.*

WORKOUT	COACH'S COMMENTS
SUNDAY	
A Rest	
B 2-mile RW at 14-16 min. pace	Focus on long strides
C 2-miles RW at 13-15 min. pace	
MONDAY	
A 2.5-mile RW at 15-16 min. pace	
B 4-mile RW at 13-15 min. pace	Focus on pushing straight back
C 3.5-mile RW at 12-14 min. pace	
TUESDAY	
A *Prekinetics* warm-up	
B *Prekinetics* warm-up	
C 4-mile RW at 13-15 min. pace	Focus on synchronized breathing
WEDNESDAY	
A 2.5-mile RW at 15-16 min. pace	
B 3-mile RW at 13-15 min. pace	Focus on walking tall
C 3-mile RW at 12-14 min. pace	
THURSDAY	
A 2-mile RW at 14-15 min. pace	
B 2-mile RW at 13-14 min. pace	Focus on quick steps
C 2-mile RW at 12-13 min. pace	
FRIDAY	
A Rest	
B Rest	
C Rest	
SATURDAY	
A Walk in the country for 1 hour	
B Walk in the country for 1½ hours	At your own pace
C Walk in the country for 2-2½ hours	

WEEK 18

WORKOUT	COACH'S COMMENTS
SUNDAY	
A Rest	
B 2-mile RW at 13-15 min. pace	Focus on synchronized breathing
C 3-mile RW at 13-15 min. pace	
MONDAY	
A 2-mile RW at 15-16 min. pace	
B 3-mile RW at 14-15 min. pace	Focus on toes pointed straight
C 3.5-mile RW at 13-14 min. pace	
TUESDAY	
A *Prekinetics* warm-up	
B *Prekinetics* warm-up	
C 4-mile RW at 13-14 min. pace	Focus on feeling your rhythm
WEDNESDAY	
A 3-mile RW at 15-16 min. pace	
B 3-mile RW at 13-14 min. pace	Focus on walking tall
C 2-mile RW at 12 min. pace	
THURSDAY	
A 2-mile RW at 15-16 min. pace	
B 2-mile RW at 14-15 min. pace	Focus on arm action
C 2-mile RW at 13-14 min. pace	
FRIDAY	
A Rest	
B Rest	
C Rest	
SATURDAY	
A Walk in the country for 1 hour	Focus on all the elements of your style
B Walk in the country for 1½ hours	
C Walk in the country for 2-2½ hours	

Have you taken your resting pulse lately? With the distance work that you have been doing, I am sure that it has been lowered considerably.

WEEK 19

WORKOUT	COACH'S COMMENTS
SUNDAY	
A Rest	Focus on recovery day, hold your form
B 2-mile RW at 13-15 min. pace	
C 3-mile RW at 13-14 min. pace	
MONDAY	
A 2-mile RW at 15-16 min. pace	
B 3-mile RW at 14-15 min. pace	Focus on synchronized breathing
C 3.5-mile RW at 13-14 min. pace	
TUESDAY	
A *Prekinetics*, warm-up	
B *Prekinetics* warm-up	
C 4-mile RW at 13-14 min. pace	Focus on your posture
WEDNESDAY	
A 3-mile RW at 15-16 min. pace	
B 3-mile RW at 14-15 min. pace	Focus on vigorous arm swing
C 3-mile RW at 13-14 min. pace	
THURSDAY	
A 2-mile RW at 15-16 min. pace	Focus on rolling along your foot
B 2-mile RW at 14-15 min. pace	
C 1-mile RW at 12 min. pace—twice	½-mile, slow RW in between
FRIDAY	
A Rest	
B Rest	
C Rest	
SATURDAY	
A Walk in the country for 1½ hours	
B Walk in the country for 1½-2 hours	Walk at your own pace
C Walk in the country for 2-2½ hours	

WEEK 20

You must constantly remind yourself of elements of your technique.

WORKOUT	COACH'S COMMENTS
SUNDAY	
A Rest	
B Rest	
C 3.5-mile RW at 13-14 min. pace	Focus on recovery day, easy striding
MONDAY	
A 2-mile RW at 15-16 min. pace	
B 3-mile RW at 13-14 min. pace	Focus on walking tall
C 3.5-mile RW at 12-13 min. pace	
TUESDAY	
A *Prekinetics* warm-up	
B *Prekinetics* warm-up	
C 5-mile RW at 13-14 min. pace	Focus on maintaining your form
WEDNESDAY	
A 3-mile RW at 15-16 min. pace	
B 3-mile RW at 13-14 min. pace	Focus on synchronized breathing
C 3-mile RW at 12-13 min. pace	
THURSDAY	
A 3-mile RW at 15-16 min. pace	
B 3-mile RW at 13-14 min. pace	Focus on foot placement
C 5-mile RW at 12-13 min. pace	
FRIDAY	
A Rest	
B Rest	
C Rest	
SATURDAY	
A Walk in the country for 1½ hours	
B Walk in the country for 1½-2 hours	Walk at your own pace
C Walk in the country for 2-2½ hours	

For the next 4 weeks the "C" team will really increase the work load so that at the end of the period you "C" team members can enter racewalks from 3 miles up to 12 miles. You will have enough stamina to finish the races. But this is only a foundation. In order to come up with some quality performances, you will have to go through the Competitors Program.

WEEK 21

WORKOUT	COACH'S COMMENTS
SUNDAY	
A Rest	
B Rest	
C 4-mile RW at 13-14 min. pace	Focus on recovery day, easy striding
MONDAY	
A 3-mile RW at 15-16 min. pace	
B 3-mile RW at 13-14 min. pace	Focus on synchronized breathing
C 4-mile RW at 12-13 min. pace	
TUESDAY	
A *Prekinetics* warm-up	
B *Prekinetics* warm-up	
C 5-mile RW at 13-14 min. pace	Focus on rolling heel to toe-off
WEDNESDAY	
A 3-mile RW at 15-16 min. pace	Focus on maintaining form
B 3-mile RW at 13-14 min. pace	
C 2-mile RW at 11-12 min. pace	Focus on maintaining form and quick steps
THURSDAY	
A 3-mile RW at 15-16 min. pace	
B 3-mile RW at 13-14 min. pace	Focus on vigorous arm swing
C 5-mile RW at 13-14 min. pace	
FRIDAY	
A Rest	
B Rest	
C Rest	
SATURDAY	
A Walk in the country for 1½ hours	
B Walk in the country for 1½-2 hours	Walk at your own pace
C 8-mile RW at 13-15 min. pace	

If you want to take your country walks on a Sunday—rest on Monday.

WEEK 22

Try taking a train or bus out a few miles and then walking home.

WORKOUT	COACH'S COMMENTS
SUNDAY	
A Rest	
B Rest	
C 4-mile RW at 13-14 min. pace	Focus on recovery day, easy striding
MONDAY	
A 3-mile RW at 15-16 min. pace	
B 3-mile RW at 13-14 min. pace	Focus on lengthening your stride
C 6-mile RW at 13-14 min. pace	
TUESDAY	
A *Prekinetics* warm-up	
B *Prekinetics* warm-up	
C 3-mile RW at 12-13 min. pace	Focus on arms at 90-degree angle
WEDNESDAY	
A 3.5-mile RW at 15-16 min. pace	Focus on synchronized breathing
B 3.5-mile RW at 13-14 min. pace	
C 3-mile RW at 11-12 min. pace	Focus on rolling heel to toe-off
THURSDAY	
A 3-mile RW at 15-16 min. pace	Focus on foot placement, toes
B 3-mile RW at 13-14 min. pace	pointing straight ahead
C 4-mile RW at 13-14 min. pace	
FRIDAY	
A Rest	
B Rest	
C Rest	
SATURDAY	
A Walk in the country for 1½ hours	Walk at your own pace
B Walk in the country for 1½-2 hours	
C Walk in the country for 2 hours	Push a hard workout

WEEK 23

"C" Team: As you increase your mileage, you're going to have to rise earlier.

WORKOUT	COACH'S COMMENTS
SUNDAY	
A Rest	
B Rest	*You Deserve it*
C Rest	
MONDAY	
A 3.5-mile RW at 15-16 min. pace	
B 3.5 mile RW at 13-14 min. pace	Focus on walking tall
C 6-mile RW at 12-13 min. pace	
TUESDAY	
A *Prekinetics* warm-up	
B *Prekinetics* warm-up	
C 4-mile RW at 12-13 min. pace	Focus on keeping your head up
WEDNESDAY	
A 3.5-mile RW at 15-16 min. pace	Focus on synchronized breathing
B 4-mile RW at 13-14 min. pace	
C 4-mile RW at 11-12 min. pace	Focus on quick steps
THURSDAY	
A 4-mile RW at 15-16 min. pace	
B 4-mile RW at 13-14 min. pace	Focus on lengthening your stride
C 4-mile RW at 12-13 min. pace	
FRIDAY	
A Rest	
B Rest	
C Rest	
SATURDAY	
A Walk in the country for 1½ hours	Walk at your own pace; keep your
B Walk in the country for 1½-2 hours	style
C Walk in the country for 2-2½ hours	

WEEK 24

WORKOUT	COACH'S COMMENTS
SUNDAY	
A Rest	
B Rest	
C 4-mile RW at 12-13 min. pace	Focus on recovery pace
MONDAY	
A 3.5-mile RW at 15 min. pace	
B 3.5-mile RW at 13 min. pace	Focus on lengthening your stride
C 6-mile RW at 12 min. pace	
TUESDAY	
A *Prekinetics* warm-up	
B *Prekinetics* warm-up	
C 4-mile RW at 12-13 min. pace	Focus on rolling heel to toe-off
WEDNESDAY	
A 3.5-mile RW at 15 min. pace	Focus on concentrating on breathing
B 3.5 mile RW at 13 min. pace	
C 2-mile RW at 11 min. pace	
THURSDAY	
A 4-mile RW at 15-16 min. pace	
B 4-mile RW at 13-14 min. pace	Focus on vigorous arm swing
C 6-mile RW at 12-13 min. pace	
FRIDAY	
A Rest	
B Rest	
C Rest	
SATURDAY	
A 5-mile RW at 15-16 min. pace	
B 5-mile RW at 13-14 min. pace	Focus on putting it all together
C 10-mile RW at 12-13 min. pace	

Now you've done it, close to 6 months of dedicated training. What is ahead for you? What are your options?

First, I'm going to assume that you were very good about your diet and that the additional expenditure of calories due to your training program caused you to lose weight. If you feel that you have more weight to lose, stay with the team that you have been on until you reach your desired weight. But don't forget that muscle weighs more than fat, so if you have been training regularly, you will have firmed up as well. I don't believe in those weight charts that give you your ideal weight for your height and body build. You could weigh the right amount according to the charts but in reality still have too much extra fat for where *you* want to be. The look of lean athleticism—that's where it is. And you all can get there or at least approach it. You can look the best you can for your age.

The more you train, the more you will firm up. If that is your goal, then stay with the program on whatever team you choose.

If you've lost the weight and achieved that firm lean look you wanted but now are continuing to lose weight, you must experiment with your diet and/or training. You may not be eating enough. Try increasing your food intake a bit. Or you may be burning so many calories during your training sessions that you can either cut down on your mileage or take another day off. The proper balance is something you will have to find for yourself.

After 24 weeks of coaching, training schedules and constant reminders on how to focus in on your body and all the elements of proper racewalking technique, you should have developed a smooth and efficient racewalking style. For you "C" team members, there is more ahead for you in the wonderful world of competitive racewalking.

For you "A" and "B" team members, there should be much renewed pride in your body, knowing where you were, what you have now achieved, and what you can achieve as a lifetime athlete. Whoever said it was so right: "If you have your health, you have everything." Athletes live longer, healthier lives. One study showed that champion cross-country skiers in Finland lived 7 years longer than the rest of the population.

When there is a lot of snow on the ground and I can't racewalk, I really enjoy cross-country skiing. It is a great sport and a great conditioner, a lot like racewalking. Try it. I have been doing it for 5 years now and have competed in a few races. That is a tough sport! My friend, Bob Falciola of the Shore AC racewalking team, has competed in many cross-country ski races including a 100 mile race.

The way to a longer, healthier life is very simple. Eat the proper foods, get sufficient rest, and exercise vigorously. Twenty-four weeks is only the beginning, but see how good you feel even now! "A" and "B" team members can continue these schedules, or some that you yourself make up, for many years. You have learned the basics. You are accomplished in your sport. Now carry on your training for life—*for your life*. Be a Lifetime Athlete.

12

COMPETITIVE RACEWALKING
A Tough Breed

In February of 1945, I won the intramural 1 mile run on the 32-laps-to-the-mile indoor track at DeWitt Clinton High School in New York City. I've been hooked on competition ever since. Actually, I finally had found something that I was good at. I was too small for the football team, too short for basketball, too weak for wrestling, and like a piece of lead in the pool. Around my neighborhood, the only reason they picked me for touch football was because I was faster and shiftier than the others, and I had a pretty good pair of hands. (The only thing was, I *really* wanted to be the quarterback.) When they picked sides for baseball and basketball, I was always picked last, but if the sides were uneven, I had to wait for another player. Talk about being left out! But after my race, all of a sudden I was walking around my neighborhood with my Clinton H. S. Track Team sweat jacket on and getting Gees and Wows! It wasn't football but I said to myself, I'll take it. I really felt good about myself.

It has been 35 years now, and I still love to compete. Basically I really hate to get beaten. The only thing is that around my 40th birthday (when I actually think that I started to grow up), I found out that even though I didn't win a race, I wasn't losing. I was still winning. There was a sense of achievement, of a job well done, of doing the best that I could, and of doing things during my training and racing which were good for my body and my mind. Then it came to me: I was creating my own youth! I look younger and feel younger. Experts at Columbia University have said that physiologically I have the body of a 20 year old. Training and competing have done it for me.

Most people who are into athletics at all have an innate sense of competition. It is really interesting to watch the stragglers in a running race or a racewalk. During the last 100–200 yards you usually see competitors expending their last bit of energy so that they *won't* be the last one to finish. That's fine. That's good, healthy competition. Those of us who compete do so for various reasons: to re-create our own youth, to experience the happening, the camaraderie, the excitement of competition, to experience a sense of achievement, to test ourselves.

Whatever your reason or reasons, don't think that you can compete without the proper training. You are in a different league now —one that requires a good mix of technique and training with a bit of caution added to the recipe.

First, the note of caution: The "C" team is the competitive team. You have enjoyed that designation for the past 12 weeks, but you haven't raced! That is because up until now you have not been ready. Now you are ready for *some* racing but only in a limited way. I don't want you to bite off more than you can chew. Injuries among racewalkers are rare. There are reasons for that. It is because we combine proper usage of technique with the proper training for the various distances at which we race. You are cleared for races from 4 miles to 12.4 miles (20 kilometers). For the next 3 months, I don't want you in any sprint races (1–3 miles) or in any distance races over 20 kilometers. It would be traumatic to your system to try and race either sprints or longer races. The conditioning that you have undergone during this past 24 weeks, especially the past 12, will support you for that mid-range of races of 4–12.4 miles but nothing on either side of that spectrum. Be patient. Play it safe.

But before we go into the next training phase for you to become a competitive racewalker, it's time for you to have a talk with yourself —a kind of reaffirmation of what your goals are and whether you have the stuff to handle what it takes to get there. Do you remember that list I gave you once before when I asked you to consider being an athlete? Well, here it is again:

- Desire
- Dedication
- Discipline
- Determination

- Courage
- The willingness to work hard
- The willingness to sacrifice
- The ability to accept pain

To whatever degree you possess these qualities, it will reflect in how you perform as a competitive racewalker. If you want to keep it light, without any serious dedication, that's O.K. You can train some, play some and enjoy the "happenings"—the experience of competing. You don't really have to push yourself—simply enjoy it at your own pace. But don't make the mistake of cutting out most of your training and just racing. That can only lead to injuries, but what would be even worse would be a reduction of your fitness level. Find the balance between training and racing that suits you.

Most people who race seriously are afflicted (and I don't mean it derogatorily) with a "pursuit-of-excellence syndrome." They are constantly seeking to improve their racing times and to upgrade their positions in the overall standings. That really is what keeps us all

I wonder which one I'll win today. Ron Daniel and Ron Kulick pass the trophy table as they compete in the annual Captain Ronald Zinn Memorial Racewalk.

James C. Wiest

going. So if you think that you are, or want to be, a serious race-walker, then I suggest that you reflect again on those qualities necessary for your pursuit of excellence.

Are you with me? Fine. Let's get to it!

In the chapter called The Technique of Racewalking, you were first "walked through" the technique, breaking down each movement in detail. On pages 114–115, the sequential action shots detailed the technique again. At this time I feel that it is important for a review of the elements of racewalking technique, making you aware that there are refinements of *competitive* racewalking technique as compared to the racewalking technique which I advocate for fitness racewalkers.

Foot Placement: Pointing the toes straight ahead and pushing straight back during the propulsive phase of the stride are musts for maximum acceleration and minimum loss of distance (review technique on pages 106–108). Desirable gait width varies with the walker's speed and balance. For competitive racewalking, I advocate a narrower gait width than heretofore mentioned. Illustrated are examples of near-optimum and optimum gait width which are additional elements enabling the racewalker to achieve maximum stride length.

Competitive Racewalking Foot Placement

Direction of travel

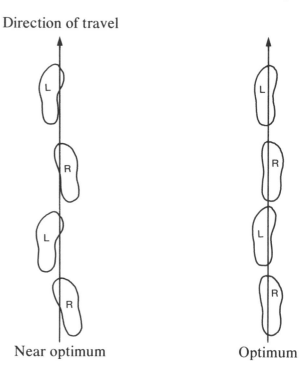

Near optimum   Optimum

In the near optimum, the feet just overlap the line of direction. Optimum foot placement is when one foot is placed directly in front of the other. It is necessary to have good hip flexibility to achieve this, and it is hip action that makes racewalkers seem "funny" to spectators who have no appreciation or understanding of what's going on. They'll learn, and even if they don't, *you* already know. Special exercises are shown on pages 170–172.

Supporting Leg Action—Contact, Mid-Stance and Propulsion: The forward leg at the end of its swing is almost fully straightened. The foot is at a 90-degree angle to the leg, anticipating heel strike. As the outside corner of the heel makes contact with the ground, that leg becomes the support leg. On contact, the ankle should be locked at an angle just wide enough to permit rolling along the outside edge of the shoe until reaching the ball of the foot for toe-off. The leg should simultaneously straighten immediately on contact, almost to the point of locking the knee so that the locked ankle and locked knee make a rigid lever of the leg. As a rigid lever, the leg is used to pull the body forward over the leg to mid-stance. This will also be helped by considerable forward momentum. Once the body is over the leg, that leg can continue rolling onto the toe for propulsion (toe-off). By rolling right up onto the toe rather than leaving the ground at the ball of the foot, you gain a precious 2 or 3 inches. To achieve maximum acceleration, it is essential that the leg remain straightened for as long as possible. Some top racewalkers can achieve a hyperextension (bowing out at the back) of the driving leg as it thrusts against the ground, creating even greater propulsion. The emphasis on hyperextension and on the roll right up and off the toe are recommended for competitive racewalking.

Swing Leg Action: The rear leg, upon leaving the ground, has now become the swing leg. The knee begins to drive forward. The trailing foot leaves the ground in an almost vertical position after toe-off and is swung forward as low as possible. As the opposite leg reaches mid-stance, the swing leg begins to straighten. The hip is pushed forward and slightly downward, and the knee and the heel reach out for the ground.

Hip Action: As the leg swings forward, the hip on that side comes through also, sinking slightly downward. At the completion of the stride, the hip rises again to its normal position. The competitive racewalker should take particular note of this next refinement of technique. In the middle of the stride, there is an opportunity to lengthen the stride: by pushing the swing hip forward as the swing leg is pass-ing the supporting leg. This can add 4 to 6 inches to the stride. There-fore the emphasis in hip action should be *forward* so as to eliminate lateral sway. (Do it properly and it won't look "funny.") This can be illustrated as follows:

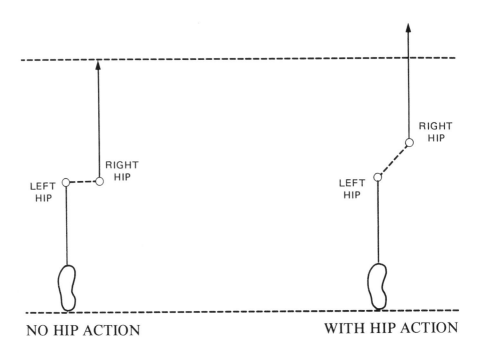

NO HIP ACTION   WITH HIP ACTION

Position of the Torso and Head: An upright posture with the feeling of "growing tall" from the back of the neck is ideal for racewalking. Presenting a higher center of gravity will also help to achieve a longer stride. Just beyond mid-stance, when the leg is braced against the ground and beginning to push, there should be a resultant slight for-ward lean of the torso but this should be no more than 5 degrees. Too great a forward lean can present difficulties in bringing through the rear leg or cause bent-knee walking which can result in disqualifica-tion. Too great a backward lean limits a walker's stride length and also causes a loss of power. Carrying the head too far forward or too far back, because of its weight and distance from the center of grav-ity, is likely to affect the whole body's balance.

Arm Action: The arms swing back and forth like a pendulum bent to 90 degrees, synchronized with the opposite leg. The loosely clenched fists cross the body slightly at mid-chest, elbows just skimming the rib cage (see again cadence breathing page 92). When the hip reaches out, it causes the hip girdle to face one plane, while simultaneously the trunk twists to accommodate the shoulder girdle, coming through with the opposite arm to face the opposite plane. This opposite rotation keeps the body's center of gravity stable, establishing good balance. The arm and shoulder movement helps to maintain the walker's stride and tempo. More usage of the shoulder can help the competitive racewalker avoid arm fatigue.

The sequence of pictures demonstrates techniques used by the competitive racewalker especially for distances of 20 kilometers down to the sprints. The refinements of technique are slight as compared with racewalking at slower speeds but if put together properly, will considerably improve your performances.

Fig. 1: This shows the left heel strike with the ankle and knee locked and pulling back hard with the quads. The right shoulder has rotated forward with the arms in a controlled swing closer to the chest so as to make an even shorter pendulum. The right knee is driving forward, and the rear foot has left the ground in a near-vertical position.

Fig. 2: The body is at mid-stance, the left foot braced against the ground. The arms are close in, moving in short quick strokes.

Fig. 3: The torso has good forward lean. The driving leg is still hyperextended as the foot has already started to raise onto the toe. The right hip has pushed forward (note the position of the stripes on the shorts), and the knee is reaching out with the foot relaxed. The arms are still at a 90-degree angle and controlled.

Fig. 4: There is still a slight forward lean. (Again, this is accomplished by "feeling" the lean from the ankles up.) The left leg has pushed all the way onto the toe (you can still see the calf muscles working). The right hip is still pushed way forward with the quads relaxed as the leg is almost straight, the foot at a 90-degree angle to the leg, ready for heel strike. The left shoulder has

come forward making a good
line all the way from the left
leg to the left shoulder. The
arms are at a 90-degree angle
and are in tight toward the
chest. The head is still erect as
it has been throughout.

Fig. 5: The right leg is pulling against
the ground and the left knee
driving forward. The body is
erect and the arms, still at 90
degrees, swing in a tight arc.

Fig. 6: The right knee is hyperextended and about to begin
pushing. The left knee is driving forward, but now the ad-
ductor muscles and quadriceps
are beginning to lift and extend the leg forward. The arms
are still in tight, and the right
shoulder is beginning to rotate
forward. The body is starting
to lean forward as a result of
its momentum and the beginning push of the right leg.

Larry Young showing excellent racewalking technique. With one foor directly in front of the other, the right outside corner of the heel is being "planted" while he is pushing straight back with the left foot. The arms are at right angles and cross to the mid-chest. Note the lack of hip sway.

Don Johnson

One way to practice accomplishing the "in tight" feeling of the very short arm stroke is to walk quickly with both palms placed directly on your breastplate, elbows close to your sides. You must concentrate on moving your hips quickly. As a result, you will feel the rotation of your shoulders. Now, close your fists and keeping your same hip action, synchronize your "in tight" arm action with your legs. You find that you are using short pistonlike strokes. You have to experiment to find that control. The Mexican walkers exhibit an extreme shoulder rotation which helps with the extension of the opposite hip and saves the arms from working too hard. The Russians use a bit more of a controlled arm movement without as much rotation of the shoulder. In Figure 3, my arms drifted just a bit too far from my chest. In Figure 4, my left arm appears high, but it is borderline. Paul Nihill, the European 20 km champion of 1969, uses a similar arm action as does Daniel Bautista, the Olympic champion and world record holder at 20 kilometers. Employing an even higher

Number 301 is the late Captain Ron Zinn, killed in action in Vietnam, July 7, 1965. Number 311 is 3-time Olympian Bruce MacDonald ('56, '60, '64), who has the distinction of never dropping out of a race. That's guts!

Eli Attar

arm action was the late Captain Ron Zinn, two-time U.S. Olympian and one-time holder of the world indoor 1 mile racewalk: 6:18.3, March 10, 1962. A danger of having too high an arm action is that it could tend to pull you upward rather than forward. This could pull you off the ground altogether and that would be illegal. There is a "fine line"; you just have to learn to stay below it.

There are certain exercises that will help you develop your race-walking technique. In addition to the *Prekinetics* and the cool-down exercises that promote general flexibility, there are special exercises that have been developed for the racewalker which will help develop shoulder and hip flexibility. Tension and tightness anywhere in the body, even the face, affect other parts of the body and, of course, performance.

Do these exercises as part of your warm-up or during an easy workout. Do each particular exercise for 50–100 yards at a time.

Front Crossover: With the fingers clasped together in front of the chest, start walking with an exaggerated crossover step as if the outside edge of the foot would be even with or over the line of the outside edge of the other foot. The arms and shoulders should swing opposite to the hip girdle. Exaggerating the movement will give added flexibility to the shoulders, torso and hips.

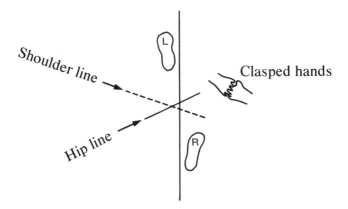

Side Crossover: This is a variation of the front crossover except that now you turn the shoulder sideways and look back over your shoulder at your trailing foot. After 25–50 yards turning to the right, turn to the left and so on.

Backward Windmill: Alternating first the right arm, then the left arm, swing the arms backward, keeping the elbows as straight as possible and as close to your ears as possible. Walk forward with one stride to one swing of the opposite arm. Excellent for the shoulders.

Strengthening Exercises: Here are a couple of great exercises for strengthening the feet.

1. Since you get your propulsion by pushing off your toes, the stronger your feet and toes are, the more you can push. Stand near a wall you can touch for balance, and raise yourself on your toes as high as you can go. Hold for 15–20 seconds. Repeat a few times.

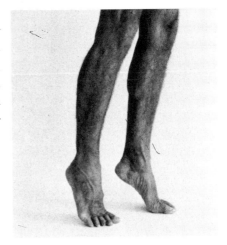

2. You also will be coming down on
   your heels and rolling along your
   foot to push off. Walk on the extreme outside edge of your feet for
   3–4 minutes.

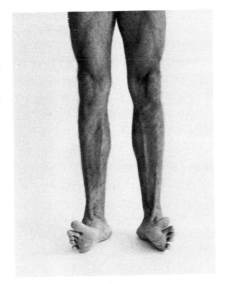

Special Technique for Hills: Racewalking uphill takes a special
technique. Because your center of gravity changes when you go up
or down a hill, as opposed to walking on the flat, you must make
necessary adjustments in your stride and arm carriage. For both
uphill and downhill racewalking, your forward momentum should be
used to optimum advantage.

As you approach an uphill, shorten your stride slightly. By adapting a shorter stride you can lean forward from the ankles, into the
hill, so that you don't lose much momentum. When your heel makes
contact with the ground, pull back hard, straightening your knee and
making a rigid lever. Make sure that that same leg pushes forward,
rolling all the way onto the toe so that you lift yourself up the hill.
Keep your arms just a bit lower and drive them with short strokes
into the hill ahead of you. Push a few yards past the crest of the hill
before lengthening your stride again.

Downhill walking actually presents more of a problem because
your center of gravity is more forward, and that can tend to pull you
off the ground, resulting in disqualification. If you maintain your
same long stride, you can take advantage of gravity and your forward
momentum, but you don't want to lose contact. Keeping the long
stride, lean forward slightly to remain almost perpendicular to the
hill. With your longer stride you will, at the double-support phase, be
closer to the ground. Allow your lead hip to drop slightly more than

usual and feel for the ground with your heel. Lower your arms slightly to keep them from pulling you off the ground. When you reach the flat, just raise your arms back to normal and keep going.

Hill training can be a great strength builder. It can be both aerobic (with oxygen) and anaerobic (without oxygen). If you train on a hilly course and take the hills as they come, breathing deeply, you can really feel it in the backs of your legs and your buttocks. Out in Westbury, Long Island, we had a hill that was 600 yards long and a mile and a half from the finish line. We made it a practice to "belt" that hill. Invited guests could challenge us to see who would be King of the Hill for that day. When we needed extra hill work, we sometimes did eight or ten repeats up that hill. That is where things become anaerobic. About half to three-quarters of the way up, after doing a few, the "bear" would jump on your back and ride up with you. But it works—so find a hill, even if it is only 50–70 yards, and do hard repeats up it. Tired you'll be, but strong you'll get.

PROFILE OF A CHAMPION
Todd Scully

Holder of two world's indoor racewalking records, Todd Scully hasn't missed a day's training in 9 years. Todd, born September 13, 1948, started out as a runner at Somerville High School in New Jersey. He graduated from Lynchburg (Va.) College with a B.S. in Chemistry and a Master's Degree in Physical Education. He ran very creditable times like 49:5 for the quarter and 1:58 for the half. As a member of Elliott Denman's Shore A.C., Todd started serious racewalking in 1971 when he was in the U.S. Army with Gary Westerfield, my Long Island A.C. teammate and protégé. I was fortunate to have some early influence on Todd with respect to technique when he came home on leave with Gary. They would report back with new training schedules derived from our consultations.

By 1972 Todd was the alternate on the Olympic 20 km team. He won his first national championship in 1975 in blistering 96-degree heat at the 40 kilometer championship with an excellent 3:21 performance. He says that he is not affected too much by heat and believes in taking liquids before and often during a hot weather race.

Volume is the answer to his training, for he puts in as much as 150 miles per week for long periods before reducing the load and sharpening with speed work. Todd has great desire and a willingness to work hard. He is a vegetarian and occasionally fasts to cleanse his body.

Currently coaching track and cross-country at Virginia Tech, he is not always able to get to certain racewalks. In December of 1978, he ran the Charlotte, N.C., Marathon in 2 hours, 36 minutes. A member of the 1976 Olympic team at Montreal, Todd is already in a program toward making his second Olympics. His recent world records in the indoor 1 mile of 5:55.8, and 12 minutes 35 seconds flat in the 2 mile, had the crowds to their feet in Madison Square Garden. He has the speed. Now he needs the strength. I think he's going to make it.

Todd is a confident young man, yet a true and modest champion. He is a good coach who understands running and racewalking. He is well liked and relates well to his athletes.

The author and Todd Scully in the 50 kilometer trials for the 1971 Pan American Games.

Alison Tores

Now would be a good time for some races. They will be good experiences. I'm sure you will enjoy them. It will also be a way to find out just how fast you can racewalk. Here is how to go about getting into some races. Write your local chapter of the following organizations:

The Walkers Club of America
The Amateur Athletic Union
The Road Runners Club

Be sure to include a self-addressed envelope with your request. Any one of these organizations should be able to put you in touch with some active racewalkers or tell you about upcoming racewalks. The New York Road Runners Club under the leadership of Fred Lebow has made it a policy to include a racewalking section in all RRC races.

If there are not very many racewalks in your area and you don't want to travel very far to get some competition, sign up for some of the running races and racewalk them. Ron Laird, one of America's greatest racewalkers of all time and member of four Olympic teams racewalked in many a road run or marathon, 20 or so years ago when there were few racewalks.

So you've sent in your entry and tomorrow is the race. Let's say 5 or 10 miles. It doesn't matter. Plan on eating dinner about 6 or 7 o'clock this evening. Don't eat anything out of the ordinary for your diet and don't eat a heavy meal. You don't have to skip dessert or a caffeine-free beverage. Later in the evening, you could have some fruit, but don't snack too much and see if you can get a good night's sleep. Don't worry about tomorrow. Just lie still and try to sleep. If you are excited about tomorrow's race, it's very normal. I'm not suggesting that you be blasé about the whole thing, for it is a great new experience. Just remain as relaxed as possible.

Today is the day. If the race is at 10 or 11 o'clock, I usually sleep until 7 or 8 A.M., get up and have a cup of tea with honey. Then I go to the bathroom and "clean myself out." I really like to "race on empty." Some people wake up ravenously hungry in the morning. Control it if you can. Otherwise, a slice of dry toast with some jelly and tea or coffee should suffice. Give yourself 2 hours before the race to digest even that. Don't make the mistake of eating a big breakfast. You'll feel loaded and you will probably have to make a pit stop. Nutritionally, what you have been eating all along up until even a day before will provide you with enough fuel. You don't need that last meal. It may turn out to be more of an inconvenience.

Eli Attar

PROFILE OF A CHAMPION
Ron Laird

Ronald O. Laird is one of the most successful athletes in American history. Born in 1938 he has been a top racewalker for 24 years and has represented the United States in four Olympics, two Pan-American teams and twenty-four international teams. His sixty-nine individual national AAU championships are the most that any American athlete, in any sport, has ever won. Laird has established eighty-one American records at various distances during his career. He has been nominated four times for the Sullivan award which is given to the outstanding amateur athlete of the year.

Ron, Bruce MacDonald, and I were teammates on the New York Pioneer Club team which won the 10 km national racewalking championship in May of 1957, my first season of racewalking. Laird was the first athlete I had encountered who was experimenting at that time with two-a-day workouts and with vegetarianism. With plenty of hard work, Ron went on to make his first Olympic team in 1960. Vegetarianism and the alfalfa sprouts (a good vegetable source of protein) that Ron was always talking about have only recently become popular. Because he took jobs only if they fit in with his training schedule and made racewalking so important in his life, many people think him odd and irresponsible. Double workouts, alfalfa sprouts, doing what you love to do —I think Ron has been ahead of his time. To me, he's a racewalker. He's a brother. The racewalker's day will come.

Do you have all of your gear washed and ready? Are you prepared for the weather? Are there dressing and shower facilities at the race? If not, take a towel and a dry T-shirt and, in winter, another turtleneck. Ask yourself if you have everything in your bag. Make a checklist:

competitive shirt   Vaseline
shorts   extra safety pins
jock   wristwatch
bra   sun glasses with elastic strap
underpants   wrist band
turtleneck   head band
leotard or long johns   kerchief
socks for your feet   toilet paper
socks for your hands or gloves   rain suit
sun cap or wool cap   warm-up suit or jacket and old
shoes   pants
towel   extra T-shirt
soap   extra turtleneck
Band-Aids   lock

Do you have a plastic bag in which to put your wet towel and/or wet shirt and shorts? Put some fruit and a can of juice in your bag, too. Did you check in before, or do you have to pick up your number at the race? Call up the weather bureau to find out the temperature and the wind-chill factor. That will help you decide what gear to bring. More about dressing for the weather later.

Arrive at the race site about an hour to an hour and a quarter before race time so that you can find a parking spot and a locker (if provided). Check in and pick up your number if you haven't already done so. Put your number on your shirt immediately so that you don't misplace it. They've run out of safety pins but you have some in your bag, right? If your husband or wife or friends or children are with you, then you know that you've got someone to hold your bag and warm-up outfit (in case there are no lockers). You might put all of your things in the trunk of your car just prior to race time. So you've got that worry off your head. Your belongings will be taken care of.

About 40 minutes before the race, begin with your *Prekinetics* stretching exercises. Do them thoroughly for about 20 minutes. This is an innovation which I started a few years ago—stretch first, then do some easy walking and fast straightaways. When I first started running, I was told to take my warm-up which consisted of a 1 or 2 mile jog, followed by some stretching exercises. Most runners and racewalkers still start with the jogging or easy walking before they stretch. Many of them exert so much energy during the warm-up that they don't have enough left for the race. I feel that it is better to stretch really well, then do a little easy walking, followed by some fast straightaways of 50 to 60 yards.

Twenty minutes of stretching, 10 minutes of easy striding and straightaways, and 10 minutes for a last trip to the bathroom or bushes and to strip down and hand your gear to someone or put it somewhere safe yourself. Walk over to the starting line and place yourself near the back of the pack. Do some fast exhalations (hyperventilate), remain calm and wait for the starter's gun.

This is it. This is reality. This is the moment of truth. Your first race and you are going to do just fine. You are well trained. You are well rested. You know your pace by now so don't get pulled along to too fast a start by the runners or by the faster racewalkers. This is a 5 mile race and you have covered 5 miles many times in practice. You also know that you have done it before at a 12 minute pace, covering the 5 miles, therefore, in an hour. Has it been easy or hard for you? These are questions that you have to ask yourself. But for now, be conservative. This is a new course for you and under race conditions. Many races have each mile clearly marked or they announce times at the halfway point. Plan on walking the first half of your race at your 12 minute pace and, if you feel good, to pick up the pace continually from there on until the finish line. Your primary aim should be to finish. If you do, you will win. No matter where you actually place in the race, you will have achieved a victory.

Tired? Beat? Wiped out? No? Not feeling too bad? You're not that tired? You could have pushed more the last 2 miles? O.K. Congratulations. You have done well. Next time, you'll push harder from the beginning? Well, *all right!* You're learning! You haven't cooled down yet and already you are planning your next race! Now, do some stretching, change into some dry clothes and join the others at the award ceremony. It shouldn't matter if you are going to get an award or not. A race and the award ceremony that follows are also part of a social event. Many of the races have refreshments afterward, and the atmosphere is one of congeniality. Talk to the other runners and racewalkers. You'll find most of them friendly, above average, interesting people. Perhaps if you meet some of the other racewalkers, you'll find out about some more races. You also may find a training partner for some of the longer weekend workouts where you'd be likely at times to welcome some company. Going to an award ceremony, having tea and a bagel, and mixing with men, women, children, champions, also-rans, organizers, spectators and their families is a whole lot better than any fancy cocktail party you could ever go to. There is a warmth and commonality of purpose that is infectious. I've met some wonderful people and made some lasting friendships during my many years of running and racewalking.

If you are a bit stiff or sore from the race, do some more stretching when you get home. A great relaxer is a long, hot tub bath. I couldn't always do it because I begrudged the time lost with my family. I am a family man, and many times my family had gone with me and was there to cheer me on and pass me drinks during some of the longer races. Some athletes give up competition as they begin to raise a family. I am fortunate to be in a sport in which one can compete until late in life. Some of the greatest memories that I will cherish are those of growing up with my children and of hearing and seeing them on the sidelines as I competed in races. I know that they were proud of their daddy then and they still are.

Take your bath or shower, relax and enjoy your day spent with family or friends. Get a good night's sleep. Tomorrow is another day. Reflect on your race, the people, the happening, your experiences. Do you feel good about yourself? You are an athlete—a competitive athlete. Were you satisfied with your performance? Did you finish strongly? Perhaps too strongly? Maybe you have to walk faster for the first part of the race. Believe me, if you enjoyed your experience, and I think that you did, you will be thinking about all of these things and will get even more involved with racewalking and your pursuit of excellence. You are coming along beautifully, and I am proud of you.

Let's dig in to some advanced training for serious competitive racewalkers. No successful racewalker ever made it without hard work and planning. In the United States as in most of the world, racewalking championships at various distances are held beginning in April/May through September/October. The Olympics, Pan American Games, and many international meets in which Americans participate are held during that period, even though we train and race the year round. Six months is a long time, and it would be very difficult to reach peak condition in April and maintain it through October.

Therefore, we program our training over the entire year to reach a near peak just before the major championships for our distances (naturally, the ones at which we are best) and for the qualification races for international teams. Many times these qualification trials are held concurrently with National AAU championships, usually in the early part of June. The most popular distances are the 20 kilometer (12.4 miles) and the 50 kilometer (31.0 miles), both being distances scheduled in the Olympic Games, Pan American Games, and the prestigious Lugano Cup for racewalking.

Those who make the teams continue training in order to reach a peak just before "The Games." Those who didn't make the team look to peak just before the championship in which they feel they will put in their best performance. Some racewalkers who are real contenders for spots on those teams may decide to peak for the trials, and then try to maintain that level of conditioning until the games.

Most top quality racewalkers can be classified as either 20 km specialists or 50 km specialists. It is very rare that a racewalker can be considered a prime threat in both events. If he tries to race seriously at both distances, he won't do justice to his performances in either. In 1972, however, Larry Young did set American records at both distances. The 20 km specialist will race often at 10 km, 15 km, 20 km, and occasionally move up for a 30 km effort. The 50 km specialist will race 30 km to 50 km races and occasionally move down to race 20 km. Special work is needed by each racewalker in order to achieve optimum performance at a particular distance.

I will go through a yearly training program with you, giving you full explanations for each period and a sample weekly training program for each period.

Because most racewalkers look to peak toward June or July, I will schedule the training program to start around October or November of the previous year.

My yearly training program for serious racewalkers is divided into three periods and two subperiods:

Preparation Period: 1–6 months
  Distance Work: 4 months;
  Distance/Speed Mix: 5 months
Competition Period: 5–6 months
Regeneration Period: 1 month

The Preparation Period

Distance Work: The purpose of this period is to build a strong foundation of overall endurance. The key to success for most of the world-class racewalkers is volume. You must be able to spend the time on your feet, especially if you are a 50 km racewalker. During this period there will be a lot of LSD, Long Slow Distance, which is something I learned from my friend and former teammate at NYU and Olympian in 1956, Gordon McKenzie. Another friend and former NYU teammate, Vince Chiappetta became a champion marathoner and ultramarathoner. A real workhorse! There will also be work at moderate-to-strong efforts for prolonged periods. Of paramount importance during this period is to increase your attention to technique, focus on eliminating any problem areas, and perfect your style. There will be a gradual buildup of both distance and the intensity of the workouts. Because the volume of the work will be considerable, I will include some double stretching sessions.

There may be various races scheduled during this 4-month preparation period, but that doesn't mean that you have to race in all or even any of them. You might want to pick a certain few. But don't change your training schedule around because of the races and please don't take them very seriously. You must keep a long-range view of your objectives. Many of us "train through" races at this time. That is, we don't take the day off before, nor do we even cut down the workout. We race and then many times take a 5 or 6 mile warm-down, so anxious are we to put mileage "in the bank." We have our 50 mile weeks and 100 mile weeks and 150 mile weeks—all in our pursuit of excellence. A while back, in a race in Central Park, I went through a 10 mile workout, arriving at the starting line just before the gun, and raced 10 km (6.2 miles) making a total of 16.2 miles for the day. The next day I covered 25 miles during my outing, which gave me a good start on the next week's work. Work will do it. Ask Bruce MacDonald. Ask Shaul Ladany.

The sample training schedules that follow contain different workouts for racewalkers of distinctly different abilities and goals. The NC team—National Class—are those racewalkers who have had a couple of years or more of racing experience and have aspirations to perform well in national class competition.

The "C" or competitive team are those racewalkers who have come up through the ranks of my program, or those experienced

Bespectacled Professor of Industrial Engineering, Shaul P. Ladany, survivor of a concentration camp, survivor of the 1972 Munich Olympic massacre, and world champion ultra-distance racewalker shows great determination as he survives another grueling race to finish 1st in the National 75 km Racewalk Championship in New Jersey. *Asbury Park Press photo by Herman Gerechoff*

racewalkers who don't wish to or cannot devote a lot of time to training.

The schedules do not show the *Prekinetics* or cool-down unless they are an *extra* part of a training session. But remember that they are to be done before and after every workout as usual.

Sample Training Schedule

Preparation Period: Distance Work (sample week in November)

C Team	NC Team
SUNDAY	
8 mi. RW at 11–12 min. pace	15 mi. RW at 9–11 min. pace

MONDAY	
Double *Prekinetics*	1 hr. RW at 75% effort

TUESDAY	
1 hr. RW at 75% effort	15 mi. RW at 9–11 min. pace

WEDNESDAY	
1 hr. RW at 75% effort	1 hr. RW at 75% effort

THURSDAY	
1 hr. RW at 75% effort	15 mi. RW at 9–11 min. pace

FRIDAY	
Double *Prekinetics*	1 hr. RW at 75% effort

SATURDAY	
15 mi. RW at 12–13 min. pace	25 mi. RW at 75% effort

Approximate Weekly Mileage: 38–40	85–88

The following is a suggested chart showing the gradual buildup of your mileage for the first 8 weeks of the Preparation Period. In general, Sunday, Tuesday, Thursday and Saturday are the buildup days, while Monday, Wednesday and Friday are for minimum mileage or rest. It is the consistency of effort and the gradual buildup with lesser efforts or rest in between that builds stamina.

WEEK	1		2		3		4		5		6		7		8	
	C	NC	C	NC	C	NC	C	NC	C	NC	C	NC	C	NC	C	NC
SUNDAY	6	6	7	9	8	12	8	15	10	18	10	20	12	20	12	20
MONDAY	R	5	R	8	R	5	R	5	R	5	R	5	R	7	R	10
TUESDAY	5	8	5	12	5	12	5	15	5	18	5	20	5	22	5	25
WEDNESDAY	5	6	5	9	5	10	5	10	5	10	5	10	5	10	5	10
THURSDAY	5	8	5	9	5	12	5	15	5	18	5	20	5	22	5	25
FRIDAY	R	R	R	R	R	R	R	R	R	R	R	R	R	R	R	R
SATURDAY	10	12	10	15	12	20	15	25	15	25	15	30	18	30	20	35
TOTAL WEEKLY MILEAGE	31	45	32	62	35	71	38	85	40	94	40	105	45	111	47	125

C=competitive   NC=National Class Competitor   Rest=Double *Prekinetics*

The Preparation Period

Distance/Speed Mix: After a solid foundation of distance work and concentrating on grooving your muscles for good technique, these next 2 months should be devoted to sharpening up in preparation for the upcoming racing season. Some of this will be accomplished by pushing through hard efforts of 6 to 12 miles. After your warm-up, start your workout at a moderate pace for about a mile or so until you really warm up; then push the rest of the workout. Other workouts will consist of a method of training developed by the Swedes called *Fartlek,* meaning "speed play." A Fartlek workout consists of a mix of sustained efforts at slow-to-moderate speeds, accelerations, uphill repetitions, slow and fast downhills, and occasional all-out bursts. The idea of Fartlek is to give the athlete a feeling of freedom from a regimented workout. You move as you *feel.* If you see a hill, you can charge up it, go back down and charge up again and again. You can put in a burst for 60–70 yards, and slow walk-recover for 30–40 yards, and accelerate for half a mile or so, then slow walk for 300–400 yards, and so on.

Here is an example of the mix in a 5–7 mile Fartlek workout:

1. Slow walking for 10 to 15 minutes, interspersed with the flexibility exercises shown on pages 170–172
2. Accelerations of 60–70 yards at submax effort; build up and ease down gradually
3. Bursts of 60–70 yards at max effort; build up and ease down gradually
4. Accelerations of 100–800 yards at sustained effort
5. Uphill accelerations of 30–40 yards
6. Downhill walking fast and slow
7. Moderate-paced racewalking for 10–15 minutes

Numbers 1 and 7 always remain at the beginning and end of the workout, but 2–6 can be mixed in any order according to the way that you feel.

In addition to hard efforts and Fartlek, there will also be some interval work, which is walking a number of shorter distances such as 440 yards and 880 yards at race pace, with a short interval of recovery. The idea of the shorter recovery period is to maintain the pace even though you are becoming progressively more tired with each interval. Taking shorter and shorter recovery periods theoreti-

Sample Training Schedule

Preparation Period: Distance/Speed Mix (sample week in February)

C Team	NC Team
SUNDAY	
Race 10–15 km or hard time trial	20 km specialist—Race 10–15 km or hard trial 50 km specialist—Race 20–30 km or hard trial
MONDAY	
1 hr. RW at 75% effort	20 km specialist—1 hr. RW at 75% effort 50 km specialist—1½-2 hr. RW at 75% effort
TUESDAY	
Double *Prekinetics*	20 km specialist—2 mi. RW, 12 x 880 race pace, 1 mi. RW 50 km specialist—2 mi. RW, 12 x 880 race pace, 1 mi. RW
WEDNESDAY	
5–7 mi. Fartlek	20 km specialist—2 hr. RW, 75% effort with accelerations 50 km specialist—3 hr. RW, 75% effort with accelerations
THURSDAY	
2 mi. RW, 5 x 880 at race pace, 1 mi. RW	20 km specialist—5–7 mi. Fartlek 50 km specialist—5–7 mi. Fartlek
FRIDAY	
Double *Prekinetics*	20 km specialist—1 hr. RW at 75% effort 50 km specialist—1 hr. RW at 75% effort
SATURDAY	
10–15 mi. RW at 75% effort	20 km specialist—20 mi. RW at 75% effort 50 km specialist—30 mi. RW at 75% effort
Approximate Weekly Mileage: 37–40	20 km: 66 50 km: 92

cally eventually brings you to eliminating them altogether and covering the whole distance at that pace (in a race). Your body adapts to the work load. This type of workout not only helps to build speed but also helps in your judgment of pace. This type of work should preferably be done on a track, but if you don't have one nearby, then any flat-surfaced parking lot or shopping center, or even going around the block will do. You could even mark off a section of the road that you train on.

At this point the 20 km specialist and the 50 km specialist will have to go their separate ways for certain of their respective training sessions. They can, however, train together for some workouts which don't require specialization. If you are fairly new to racewalking competition and are on the "C" team, stick to the 20 km training. Most of you are not yet ready to move up to the long one.

During this period, particular attention must be paid to your technique so that the faster walking doesn't lead to style problems.

Dave Romansky is one of the strongest racewalkers I have ever known. His fierce drive and intense competitive spirit are matched by his ability to push himself during training. His 80–100 miles per week training schedule is based on a big percentage of quality workouts, at or near all-out efforts. In his week, Dave gets in one moderate-paced 25 mile session, one 18 mile all-out, and two sessions of interval work on the track. The rest are moderate-to-hard 10–12 mile workouts. On the track he will do 40 x 220 yards all out, each one with a 110 yard rest interval between, where he walks slowly, or 20–30 x 440 yards all-out, each one with a 110 yard rest interval between. Then he will do run-ups of the stadium steps, followed by an all-out run of 2–4 miles. No wonder he has such strength. He goes after it!

Competition Period

A racewalker will learn only by racing at different distances. In that way, you will find out which distances suit you best. You will also be able to assess your condition and see what you need to put you into top condition. You might be short on endurance for certain distances, in which case you would add to your mileage and the quality of your workouts. You might be in need of speed work if you finished the race, not having fully expended your energy, but just didn't have the leg speed to take you through that fast pace. Strategy during the race is another thing that you can learn only by racing. Did you finish too strong and have too much left? Or did you go out too fast and have nothing at the end? Did you let the leaders go during the first half only to find that you were closing on them near the finish, but it was too late?

You should make an overall racing plan. This period is a long one (5–6 months). Your training should be flexible in order to plan at which times you will race and at which times you will train through. You should plan to peak for the championship races in your event. You may want to train yourself to a high level and maintain that level until just before the big ones and then peak. A general consensus of the top racewalkers advocates this last approach to training. It represents a good balance between training to keep you strong, and racing to keep you sharp.

Depending upon how much you race determines how much training, and the type of training, that you do during this period. Racing at distances considerably below your specialty is not going to help you when you need the strength for your big races. Therefore, you either have to train through or skip certain races, and put in your distance or do some of your distance during the middle of the week. A 20 km person can race consistently at 5, 10, 15 km and occasionally jump into a 25, 30 or 40 km race for a strength workout. The 50 km person has more of a problem. Almost all of the races are below 50 km, nor are there very many 50 km races either. So you have to avoid the lure of racing too many of the shorter races (I mean 5–20 km), and you

Sample Training Schedule

Competition Period (sample week in June)

C Team	NC Team
SUNDAY	
Race or 3 hr. RW at 75% effort	20 km specialist—Race or 4 hr. RW at 75% effort 50 km specialist—Race or 5 hr. RW at 75% effort
MONDAY	
1 hr. RW at 75% effort	20 km specialist—1 hr. RW at 75% effort 50 km specialist—1 hr. RW at 75% effort

TUESDAY	
Double *Prekinetics*	20 km specialist—2 mi. RW, 10 x 880 race pace, 1 mi. RW 50 km specialist—2 mi. RW, 15 x 880 race pace, 1 mi. RW
WEDNESDAY	
2 mi. RW, 6 x 880 at race pace, 1 mi. RW	20 km specialist—1 hr. RW at 75% effort or Fartlek 50 km specialist—2 hr. RW at 75% effort or Fartlek
THURSDAY	
5–7 mi. Fartlek	20 km specialist—2 mi. RW, 12 x 440 race pace (90% effort), 1 mi. RW 50 km specialist—2 mi. RW, 12 x 440 race pace (90% effort), 1 mi. RW
FRIDAY	
2 mi. RW, 6 x 440 at race pace (90% effort), 1 mi. RW	20 km specialist—1 hr. RW at 75% effort 50 km specialist—1 hr. RW at 75% effort
SATURDAY	
Double *Prekinetics*	20 km specialist—Double *Prekinetics* 50 km specialist—Double *Prekinetics* (You may reverse Friday and Saturday)
Approximately Weekly Mileage: 37	20 km: 60 50 km: 72

have to stick to your training plan. However, if there aren't enough distance racewalks in your area, you can jump into a runner's marathon and racewalk it.

For the 20 km racewalker who is really looking to develop leg speed, I advocate a lot of 150-yard, all-out sprints. But even during these repeats, you must maintain your form. They need not be timed because the all-out effort is what counts. Do as many as you can until you are rubber legged. It is really hard anaerobic (without oxygen) work. Be sure to do a 2-mile warm-up before and at least a 1-mile cool-down afterward. A Thursday or a Friday is a good day to do them if you are going into a short race on Sunday.

Before major races, adjust your training and racing schedule so that you are at your strongest and sharpest. Before a 20 km championship, some of the top racewalkers like to race a 10 km the week before and lighten up on their work load during that week. They do some speed work and easy striding so that they are rested and ready.

In the 50 km event, it is advisable to have the last hard race 2 weeks before, and then only at a distance of no more than 20 km. You can't race at 50 km every week or every 2 weeks. An ideal schedule would be no more than once a month or even 6 weeks. The body has to have time to recover from hard efforts at 40–50 kilometers. This is no different than if you were a marathon runner. The marathon distance is approximately 42 kilometers, and many of the top marathon runners will run only 5 or 6 marathons a year.

There are some top racewalkers who rarely, if ever, take a day off. Their training regimen has enabled their bodies to adapt to the constant work load. Some don't even take the day off before a major race. There are others who take Friday off if they are racing Sunday and take a very light workout on Saturday. Other racewalkers always take a day off each week regardless of a racing schedule. This becomes a matter of the individual's preference and how he or she can adapt to certain work loads. As much as improvement is a matter of training and application, it is also a matter of nutrition and sufficient rest. The overtrained athlete will soon become stale and unable to perform.

After a really hard race, you may be stiff and sore the next day. You may not feel up to training. That is the day you really need it. Push yourself to take a double *Prekinetics* and an easy ½ to 1 hour walk. Then take the following day off if you need it. The easy stretching and easy walking accelerate recovery from those hard efforts by getting the body's systems going again and increasing the circulation which will allow the oxygenated blood to carry off the waste products of the effort.

All your training and the best of diets with plenty of rest won't do you a bit of good unless you have a race plan. Racewalking is an endurance event, and you must therefore spread your energies out over the entire distance of the race. If you go out too fast, you'll pay for it later. If you go out too slowly, you'll lose contact with the leaders and won't be able to make it up later. If you fall asleep during a middle phase of the race—same thing—you'll lose contact. What is the answer? The answer is that you must race to find out what shape you are in. By that I mean how fast you can go the whole way for a given distance. You must also know your competition and how fast they can go. If you are close in ability to someone, you should race with that person to help pull you through the race. In each race, there will be only one winner, but there may be a few people in the race capable of winning it. Each one has his own race plan for winning. Behind the leaders are those who won't win but will score well. They too have a plan. There are, therefore, a number of different strategies that one can employ in racing:

STRATEGIES PLANNED TO WIN THE RACE

1. Set a fast pace from the gun, feeling that you can maintain that pace to the finish, but the rest of the field cannot. Some might try to hang on for portions of the race but will fall away one by one.
2. Set a very fast pace from the outset and burn off the competition, then settle down to walk your own race. The big danger of this is that you may burn yourself out and not be able to keep the lead later.
3. Walk with the leaders, hanging in there until you see an opportunity to make your sprint move. It might come down to the last ½ or ¼ mile, and you must worry about being super legal.

STRATEGIES PLANNED FOR BEST POSSIBLE PERFORMANCE

1. Walk your own race. You have a pretty good idea of your ability so the best thing to do is to stick to a time schedule for the first ½ to ¾ of the race, and if you are feeling good, pick it up to the finish. If you are feeling bad, *C'est la vie!*

2. If you are feeling up, you can latch on to someone who is just a bit better than you for as long as you can. You may surprise yourself and him too.

Walking shoulder to shoulder or a stride length behind someone is a battle of wits as well as a physical thing. If you are the favorite and have had consistently better performances than your rival, there are a number of thought processes that may go through your head. If the pace has been fast and he's there after ¼ to ½ of the race, you don't worry very much. If the race gets to the ¾ mark and he's still there, you start to think, What kind of training has *he* been doing? You glance over at his face and look for signs of distress—heavy breathing or strain. You might decide to throw in a burst up (or down) the next hill, or just pick up the pace to see if he goes with you. If he does and is still there, expect a battle to the tape but try to pick up the pace again and look to shake him well before the final stretch. There are times when you don't feel like pushing too much faster at that stage, so you might wait until the last mile before really turning it on. Just take off at that point and drive toward the finish line. You may shake him immediately.

At the '68 Games, Paul Nihill (the '64 Silver Medalist in the 50 kilometer racewalk) and Larry Young of Great Britain were at lunch the day before their race discussing how they were going to walk. Nihill said he was going for a 4 hour, 10 minute time and anyone trying to beat him would have to walk faster than that. Larry said he was going to walk his own race and that he might see Nihill around the 40 km mark. The race was in Mexico City, and Larry had had experience training at altitude so he was going to be conservative in the beginning. Nihill was fading badly as Larry passed him at 35 km. The race was slow, as are most distance performances at altitude. Christoph Hohne of East Germany won in 4:20:13, Antal Kiss of Hungary was second in 4:30:17 and Larry Young was third in 4:31:55.

In a longer race, if your opponent has to make a pit stop, you may be able to put enough distance between you so that he'll never catch you, but there can be a danger in that, too. If it's too early in the race and you picked up the pace too much, you may pay for it later.

There are many times when simply walking your own pace will pay off with your best time or a good place in the order of finish. The best time is when the leaders have killed each other off, and you can pass them and go on to win.

If winning is as important to you as it is to some of us, then you have to develop your mind as well as your body. To win you must be able to take risks. If you are well trained and strong, take the risk. Each risk you take and each resultant improvement you make will mark a personal win for you even when you don't take first place.

Walking around a flat indoor track with tight turns can be quite an art. Since you are moving at a fast pace, centrifugal force will tend to pull you away from the inside of the track. Take a lesson borrowed from the sprinters and pump your right arm with your leg speed, but control your left with very slight pistonlike strokes, and you will counteract the force. Resume your normal arm swing as you come off the turn. The same thing should be done on a steeply banked track with tight turns, but there it won't take as much effort to stay "on course."

When attempting to pass someone, whether on a road or a track, pass decisively so that you don't give a rival a chance to wake up and surge with you. Just make sure that if you are passing, you don't cut in front of him, causing him to stop short or trip over you. You might go down, too.

Regeneration Period

After a long season of hard training and racing, most athletes need a physical and mental rest. Racewalkers are no different, with the exception of a few workaholics who hardly, if ever, take a day off. The training is physically demanding while the racing is pressure filled. We need some diversion, some time off. We need to play and we need to rest. We have to get away from schedules, perhaps to participate in some activities that we can't do while we are in training. But here's the catch: We can't just rest completely. The high level of fitness that has been achieved must not be allowed to decline too far because it would then be too difficult to get back into shape after the period is over. Therefore, a light training schedule is the answer. The regenerative benefits come from not having to race, although we love to race, and not putting in a heavy volume of work. Sleeping late is of restorative value, but equally so is being able to swim or play ball or go dancing. Resting too much drives most athletes bananas anyway, so they are eager to get back to a normal training routine. The rest and the diversion have, however, accomplished their purpose: We are recharged and ready to resume training.

That, then, is a yearly training program for a competitive racewalker. It is, of course, only a guide. You will have to experiment and find out what works best for you. Some racewalkers thrive on racing, building their training programs to include many races. Others prefer not to race often, concentrating on heavy training. I believe that you should train more and race very little in the preparation period but let the races keep you in shape during the racing season.

Steve Hayden on the track at the Bisslet Invitational 10,000 meters in Oslo, Norway, 1972.

PROFILE OF A CHAMPION
Steve Hayden

Born in Brooklyn, in 1944, Steve and his family moved to Wantagh, Long Island, where he was enrolled at Wantagh High School. Although a solid runner in the mile and 2 mile, his favorite was cross-country. In 1961 Steve was the New York State cross-country champion.

He first started racewalking at the Long Island A.C. development meets in 1964 while attending Penn State University. Steve graduated with a B.A. in Education in 1966 and then obtained an M.A. in Secondary Education,

Quiet and unassuming, Steve is the perfect model of the modest champion. Married to the former Women's National One Mile Indoor Racewalking Champion, Lynn Olson, they have two children and live on Long Island where Steve is a school administrator.

His best times: 10 mile—1:14
20 km—1:32:06
50 km—4:23:22

Steve Hayden says of his Olympic Trial Race, 1972:

The start of the race was as expected with Larry Young and some others taking the lead at a sensible pace. I was content to stay with the next pack of walkers, still within striking distance of the leaders. Our pace seemed very comfortable to me. Then somewhere between 15 and 20 km, a judge told me that I was walking illegally and gave me a caution. I thought, He must be mistaken; I have never felt so solid before! So I decided to leave the pack and picked up my pace in order to make myself more visible to other judges. From that point on, not another complaint was made about my style. Now I felt even better as other walkers ahead of me seemed to be having trouble—two disqualifications, a few dropouts—and I was gaining on those ahead!

By the 25 km mark, I was in 5th place and still gaining! Suddenly, it occurred to me that I had a shot at making the team. At 35 km I moved into 4th. One more man to catch! Soon the 40 km mark came up and there he was ahead of me. It was like a dream coming true. Adrenaline must have been pouring into my body, for as I passed him I could tell I was finally getting tired, but it wasn't slowing me down. During that last 5 km, there was time to reflect. All the experiences, the people, the desire that had led to this, the greatest fulfillment I had ever experienced, rushed through my mind. The finish line came up quickly, 4:23:22 from the time we started. I thanked God that 28 years of living had taught me not to give up!

THREE

The Athletic Life

13

LOOKING ATHLETIC
At Least Try to Approach It

The fashion magazines show trim, athletic-looking women. The newspapers and Sunday supplements portray American men and women of all ages, engaging in athletic pursuits. In Florida there is a senior citizens' baseball league. There are white-haired ladies and gentlemen who run marathons. At the 69th Annual Walkers Club of America Coney Island Racewalk, the oldest competitor was Dr. Edward Doran, age 82. Believe me, you can look athletic at any age.

These are athletes engaging in physical exercise on a daily basis, watching their weight. These are average people who simply decided to become athletes and now look the part. How do you think they got that way? They certainly didn't all start out as athletes or even look like athletes. Many people first started well after high school or college or even quite late in life. Whether of small, medium or large build, most men and women, at one time or another, have had thoughts of looking slimmer and more athletic. I am sure that you have, too. Well, now is your chance. I don't care if you are 17 or 77, you can look athletic at any age. Dr. Paul Dudley White, the famous cardiologist, said, "If you are in good physical condition when you are 21 years old, then you should never weigh more than you do at that age." That statement was made to remind us that most people are fairly lean at that age, and gaining too much weight can make you susceptible to degenerative diseases, especially those of the heart. Try to slip on that old wedding dress or cheerleader costume. Try to get into your old army outfit or the chinos that you wore in college. Not so easy. Right? The pounds and the inches have a way of creeping up on you through the years. *But it does not have to be that way!* If you are overweight, you can lose that weight. If you are soft and flabby, you can become firm and strong.

Strip down to naked and take a good look at yourself in a mirror. Are you fat? Answer yourself honestly. Do you have a "spare tire" or other obvious bulges? It's there, right? Now, lie flat on your back on the floor. If you put a yardstick along the center line of your body from your breastplate to your pubic bone, it should touch both. If your stomach is in the way, the ruler will ride on your stomach. Too much stomach. If your stomach is bigger than your chest, too much stomach. More than half the fat on your body is just under the skin. Stand erect, letting your arms hang free. Give yourself a pinch test by pinching with the thumb and forefinger a fold of skin at the back of your upper arm halfway between your shoulder and your elbow. That fold should measure between ¼ and ½ inch thick. If it is more than ¾ of an inch, you could lose some weight. If it is more than an inch, you are fat and should definitely get on a sensible reducing program. If you look fat to yourself, you look fat to other people as well.

Both the men and the women in my programs have lost from 10 to 40 pounds during their first year of racewalking. How did this happen? Very simply. They became athletes. They became racewalkers. They went on training programs, exercised, and if overweight, controlled their diets. They had what you need—the Desire. According to Dr. Joyce Brothers, probably the nation's best-known psychologist, "Many programs fail simply because the person simply doesn't have a strong enough *desire* to lose weight by eating less or by exercising more." In becoming athletes, my people developed attitudes that made good things happen to them. Because they *wanted* so much, they mustered up the Determination and developed the Discipline to stay with their programs.

In this chapter you will learn another approach to dieting and losing weight—one that differs from all the rest because of the attitudes and disciplines involved and because of the basic motivation toward your goal: to think and look more like an athlete. Being an athlete, if only part-time, will get you where you want to be or at least to approach it. I conservatively say "approach it" because I know where most of you are starting from. In 1978, 79 million people were reported to be dangerously overweight. According to the Metropolitan Life Insurance Company's latest figures, the average American is some 30 pounds overweight. I don't expect you all to lose weight or build your bodies so that you look like world-class racewalkers. Some of you actually will, but while most of you won't, you will all make a satisfying and certain improvement in the shape of your bodies. Most women gain their weight from their waists to their knees and also on the backs of their arms. Most men gain weight in their stomachs and behinds, especially, along the entire upper body. Not only will you lose pounds, but you will also lose inches. Your flesh will become firmer along with it. As to how closely you approach that ideal lean athletic look really depends on how hard you work mentally and physically. It depends on how far you are willing to go to feel and look good. Not everyone has to be racing slim, but you can certainly improve from where you were. When you train, you will be shaping a new you. And when you reach the point where you have shed most of the excess fat, firmed up your muscles and improved your posture, you can't help but look more athletic!

My racewalk programs and my athletes' training table ideas help you accomplish energy balance. Energy balance is associated with caloric consumption versus calorie expenditure. *Losing weight is a problem of very simple mathematics and extremely complicated discipline.* When it comes to eating, I will never minimize the difficulty of discipline. I am an ice cream freak. My father lovingly used to call me "cake face" and push another piece across the table to me. Thank God, I burned it up! I adore pasta, and I really have to watch myself when I want to be at my top racing weight. Yes, I know what discipline is. My attitudes as an athlete have helped me control my appetite. Incidentally, there is a popular myth that the more you exercise, the greater your appetite. This is just not so. Regular exercise acts as a natural appetite depressant for most people. Conversely, those involved in competitive racewalking can really develop quite an appetite so they must muster particular control. But those words—*you must be in control*—apply to anyone who aspires to cultivating a better body. Think about those words. Aren't they *the key* to behavior modification—maintaining discipline so that you don't set yourself up for a fall (going off your diet, in this case)? Your attitudes and goals as an athlete will help pull you through.

The simple mathematics of energy balance comes from the consumption and expenditure of calories. A calorie is a unit used for measuring energy produced by food when oxidized in the body. If the body does not burn up as many calories as you have eaten, the excess turns into fatty tissue. A pound of fatty tissue is the equivalent in energy of 3,500 calories. A negative energy balance means that you are burning up more calories than you are taking in, thereby losing weight. A positive energy balance means that you are taking in more calories than you are burning, thereby gaining weight. If what you burn up equals what you take in, then you have an energy balance and will keep your weight constant.

Let's imagine that you are a relatively inactive person in your early 40s. You are overweight and would like to lose 20–30 pounds. The first thing to do is to figure out how many calories a day you are now consuming. This can be done by keeping a careful record of everything you eat and drink for a week. You can get calorie counters in bookstores, drug stores or health food stores. Be sure in your computations to be careful and honest about the size portion you're eating. What and how much you eat, if you are an average-size adult, will probably add up to approximately 2,400–2,600 calories per day. If you are consuming considerably more than that, then you are really overdoing it.

Everything you do, or even don't do because basal metabolism comes into it, burns up calories at a certain rate. For a 150-pound adult, just sitting burns up about 110 calories per hour; dressing or showering 190; average office or housework 180–250; sleeping 75. A lighter person burns up slightly fewer calories per hour while a heavier person burns up slightly more. The sum total of daily activities for the average-size adult who isn't into any regular exercise program expends about 2,200–2,400 calories.

Your daily caloric intake then is in positive energy balance by 200 calories which means that in a month you will gain almost 2 pounds. If you were to eliminate that differential of 200 calories per day by cutting out 4 teaspoons of sugar and two slices of bread, for example, you would have an exact energy balance and maintain your weight. If you cut down your caloric intake by 500 more calories per day and consume only 1,700–1,900 (which is still enough to maintain proper nutrition), then you would lose about a pound per week. If you racewalk 1 hour each day at close to 12 minutes per mile, then you would burn up 500 calories more for a total of 3,500 per week, or another pound per week. That means you could burn up 7,000 calories per week, or 2 pounds, by diet and exercise. It would now take you 10 weeks to lose that 20 pounds. Simple mathematics.

Until now all of the various charts describing the caloric burn of various activities have listed walking but never racewalking. A study was done in 1979 at Columbia University by Professor Robert Gutin, head of the Department of Applied Physiology, and his assistants, Jeff Young and Dan Alejandro. The study indicates that racewalking not only will burn many more calories than walking but, at certain speeds, even more than running. This appears to be due to the more dynamic usage of the arms than in running and of the taking of more steps producing more muscular repetitions per minute.

For example:

CALORIES BURNED

MILES PER HOUR	RUNNING	RACEWALKING
5.0	480	530
6.0	660	734
7.0	690	960

These figures make racewalking fall into the category of being an absolutely excellent conditioner because of its dynamic, aerobic and endurance-building qualities. The study also contradicts earlier statements that you must walk farther in order for the calories to be burned than you would run. Actually, assuming you walk the same speed as you might run, you can walk the same distance, burn more calories, build better controlled posture and alignment, and spare the jars to your skeletal system.

It may be that you are not that much overweight and really don't need to lose weight. Remember your energy balance? Racewalking will burn a lot of calories. So possibly you won't have to reduce your caloric intake at all. In fact, you might have to eat more in order to maintain your weight!

For those of you who do have to diet, there are many offered: the rice diet, the water diet, the grapefruit diet, the fructose diet and hundreds of other "best seller" diets, all extolling the virtues of "a way to a slim, trim, more beautiful you"—and most of them are bunk. People fall for that stuff time and time again because they want to believe that there are painless, quick and guaranteed ways. We spend $10 billion a year trying to lose weight, but the sad reality is that 95 percent of those who do lose gain it right back. There is no easy way. It takes a lifetime of Dedication and Discipline. Dieting is a question of willpower, and there are no pills which will give that to you. Still every year, for decades, there has been "this year's diet" and the "newest and best" plan for weight reduction. Only now some of them are beginning to speak of exercise as a "help" in losing weight. Perhaps the diet experts, along with most of the medical profession, will wake up to the real values of vigorous exercise as a way to attain proper weight and control it, and as a way to prevent certain degenerative diseases. Weight Watchers, one of the most successful of them all, after all these years has only recently introduced its "Pep Step." It's about time. Nathan Pritikin, whom you'll soon learn more about, has gone further than any of them regarding exercise—especially walking.

Dr. D. Mark Hegsted, Director of the Government Human Nutrition Center states, "While Americans may be the best fed people in the world, that fact has caused problems for nutrition educators since you can't just tell people what to eat to keep or make them healthy, you have to motivate them, too."

I maintain that becoming an athlete is the key to new attitudes and disciplines about yourself that will motivate you to accomplish your goals of physical fitness and actually enjoy doing it. As you are gaining in endurance and allover fitness, you will most likely be losing weight. Knowing what you are seeking to achieve as an athlete and wanting to look like an athlete, you will find yourself *not* wanting to undo all the good that the exercise and diet are doing for you. One of my LIAC teammates and protégé, John Markon, is 6 feet 4 inches tall and weighed 240 pounds before he started racewalking. He smoked two packs of cigarettes a day and had high blood pressure. John is an original Renaissance man—likes baroque music, is very well read, and is amazingly well disciplined. Within 2 years he was down to 168 pounds and doing 50 kilometer and ultra-distance racewalks. He set two U.S. Masters records at 3 and 6 miles. This man was not an athlete to start with. He *became* an athlete. So can you. Just *want* it enough.

Another of Hippocrates' statements, "Thy food shall be thy remedy," has always held great truth. You don't have to be a doctor to figure that one out. A man who was diagnosed as having a coronary condition 18 years ago, which would have relegated him to a life of inactivity at age 45, is now helping people to guard against cardiovascular problems. Nathan Pritikin read all the medical literature he could locate on nutrition, exercise and degenerative diseases. He found that those countries which had a high incidence of cardiovascular disease also had diets containing high levels of fat. Those countries with a low incidence of cardiovascular disease had low levels of fat. Pritikin drastically reduced the fat content of his own diet and embarked on a daily walking program. He literally cured himself and no longer suffers from coronary insufficiency. In 1975 he opened the Longevity Research Institute, now based in Santa Monica, California, and is helping thousands of people.

The average American's present-day diet contains 40 percent fat. The American Heart Association advocates a diet containing 35 percent fat. Pritikin's diet of 10 percent fat is considered radical by some sources, but people are graduating from his Longevity Center in Santa Monica with remarkable results. In 1977 the Senate Select Committee on Nutrition recommended national dietary goals which seem to approach Pritikin's recommendations, by endorsing a diet comprised of less fat and cholesterol, more complex carbohydrates, and less simple sugar. The Committee also recommended eating fewer total calories and more vegetables and fruits in the diet. The Pritikin Program and the Senate Committee's recommendations, while primarily designed for guarding against heart disease, are also a good way to lose weight. Incidentally, there is no popular diet designed for weight loss, other than Pritikin's, which puts the emphasis on vegetables as its main staple. In terms of nutrition, however, vegetables contain more vitamins, minerals, protein and fiber, calorie for calorie, than any other food.

For a number of years I was racing at 150 to 155 pounds. My times were good and I was placing well. When I became a vegetarian, 4 years ago, I immediately lost 10 pounds and felt better than I ever had in my life. My performance times now have become even better than they were 20 years ago. I, too, read everything I can about diet, exercise, stress and degenerative diseases. I have put this knowledge to work for myself and for the people in my programs with outstanding results.

A guiding principle of the ancient Greek's life was that of moderation. I believe in it. I practice it. I don't smoke. I rarely drink hard liquor. I enjoy sex. I am "in training" every day of the year, but I eat everything I like (I just watch the quantities). I really enjoy my life.

Here is a well-balanced diet which will assure you of getting all the necessary vitamins and minerals for proper nutrition. In addition this type of diet is lower in fats, cholesterol, protein and sugars, and high in carbohydrates and fiber. Now, your exercise *and* your diet will help guard you against heart disease. For those of you interested in losing weight, you must count calories as diligently as you would your bank statement. As you progress you will realize that losing weight is a matter of mathematics. Just watch your balance.

My athlete's training table recommendations:

1. Buy a calorie counter!
2. Eat at least one serving every day from each of the following food groups so as to be sure of proper nourishment:
   - Leafy green and yellow vegetables, either raw or cooked. They contain vitamins A and C, niacin, calcium, iron, thiamine. Romaine lettuce has six times the vitamin A and three times as much calcium, iron and vitamin C as iceberg lettuce. The best way to cook vegetables is to steam them for about 5–6 minutes. They are nice and crunchy and have lost little of their nutrients.
   - Citrus fruit and two or three other fruits daily. They provide vitamins A and C, iron and calcium. Bananas are high in potassium, which together with sodium (salt) are necessary for the proper flow of fluids among and through cells.
   - Potatoes are an excellent source of carbohydrates for energy and vitamin C. The skins provide iron.
   - Whole grain breads, rice or cereals. They are rich in minerals, vitamin E and the B vitamins. They provide protein, energy and roughage.
   - Legumes, especially beans and peas, provide protein and other trace minerals such as peas for potassium, However, freezing or canning depletes their value. Fresh is still the best.
   - Low-fat cheeses and skim milk are good for calcium, vitamins A and D, and high quality proteins.
   - Polyunsaturated margarine and vegetable oils (used sparingly). Vegetable oils are rich in vitamin E and also give us essential fatty acids.
3. Modest amounts of chicken or fish are all right, but I would really stay away from meat. If you do eat an occasional piece of chicken, remove the skin which is loaded with fat.
4. Most Americans consume far too much salt. Salt causes the body to retain fluids, causing edema (swelling) which can cut down on the blood oxygen exchange between the cells and the capillaries. It has also been proven that salt contributes to hypertension which can be reduced by decreasing the salt intake. Almost all foods have some natural salt in quantities that are sufficient for most of us. So use salt very sparingly.

5. There is a lot of controversy about caffeine. It is a drug that is known to produce rapid heartbeat, high blood pressure and insomnia. It is also suspected of causing anxiety, nervousness and irritability. Caffeine is found in chocolate, cocoa, cola drinks, coffee and tea. I rarely drink soda, much preferring fruit juices and beer. Beer helps to keep the HDL (high density lipoproteins) at a high level in the blood. Some scientists believe that HDL helps to ward off atherosclerosis. It certainly is a better drink than sugar-laden soda. Besides, I like it. I have coffee once or twice a week and drink a lot of herbal tea.

6. The average man, woman and child in America eats more than 100 pounds of sugar a year. That amounts to 176,000 calories, the equivalent of over 50 pounds of body fat. If you don't burn up those calories somehow, you'll store them in your fat cells. About ¾ of the sugar we eat comes in processed foods so you can avoid sugar in two ways. First, go natural: buy fresh fruits and vegetables. Canned and frozen fruits have added sugar; canned and frozen vegetables have added salt. Some even have sugar. Second, cut down on your direct usage of sugar to sweeten drinks or cereal. Even better, cut it out. That's a surprisingly easy thing to do after the first week or so. You lose the sweet tooth you thought to be so much a part of you, and you actually find sweet things taste too sweet.

7. I have not eaten anything fried for close to 4 years now, and that includes potato chips which I used to love. Popcorn, just lightly salted and with no butter, is a surprisingly good low-calorie munchie. Frying food increases the calorie count of that food besides making it harder to digest.

8. And a basic rule in dieting: Do not allow yourself to become so hungry that you lose your willpower and begin gorging on all the wrong foods. You can eat all day if you eat the right things and watch the quantities.

A good athletic track has a white guideline painted on the inside edge in order to keep you from crossing over onto the infield during a race. The following are some behavioral guidelines for your diet which will help prevent you from "walking off the track":

- Make a shopping list and buy only what's on it.
- Do your food shopping *after* a meal. Your willpower will be at its strongest.

- Buy your fruits and vegetables first. They fill up the cart and discourage impulse buying.
- Drink water if you are angry or anxious. It's filling and calorie-free.
- Keep the refrigerator as empty as possible.
- Always break your nighttime fast with breakfast. It sets you up so that you won't be ravenous by 10:30–11:00 A.M.
- Eat the three basic meals a day. Never skip a meal.
- Always sit down and eat. Don't do it on the *walk*.
- Snack in between if you are hungry. Or drink water.
- Eat raw vegetables as snacks. Keep some with you in a plastic bag and keep the refrigerator stocked with them.
- If you snack on fruit, put it on a small plate and eat it slowly with a knife and fork.
- Use smaller plates and glasses rather than larger ones.
- Serve dinner from the kitchen onto each individual plate, not passed around family style, where there could be a temptation to overload or to come back for seconds.
- Eat very slowly and chew thoroughly.
- Don't ever keep sweet goodies around the house.
- Brown bag your lunch. Eat it at your desk and take a walk afterward.
- In a restaurant, send the bread away immediately.
- Try an herbal tea, a vitamin C, and one cookie at snack time.
- If you do go off your diet and eat some high-calorie goodies, subtract those extra calories from your next couple of meals.
- Be rigid about your portion sizes.
- Weigh yourself in the nude, before breakfast.
- Reward yourself with some new item of clothing as you lose inches.

Most of these tips you may have read or heard before. It is really common sense, isn't it? More important is the attitude with which you approach losing weight and becoming fit. Many athletes have a dream of making the United States Olympic team or of winning an Olympic medal. Have your own dream. Dream that you can be younger, fitter, slimmer than you have ever been. Then work out your dream. *Make* it come true. Athletes have such strong Desire, Dedication and Discipline that *nothing* stops them in their quest for the Olympic Gold. Whatever your "gold" is, it's attainable and waiting for you. As an athlete you can get it. And look like you got it!

14

THE CAMARADERIE OF ATHLETICS
Training, Racing, Socializing

"Friends have all things in common."

—PLATO

Reflecting on 35 years of running and racewalking, my most cherished recollections are not of any races or honors that I have won. Rather, they are of my friends and what we have shared. It wouldn't matter if it were swimming, football, lacrosse or any other sport. It also wouldn't matter if we were business executives, policemen, construction workers, teachers or whatever. Yes, birds of a feather *do* tend to flock together. Mutual interests and activities promote camaraderie—the warm, friendly feelings between friends. For us, running and racewalking were our common denominator. I think that our experiences and feelings for each other have been special. We have loved each other and most of us still do.

Some time ago some superintellectual, writing in one of the local papers, deplored the "public display of affection" between a soccer player and his teammates after he had scored a brilliant goal. "They jumped on him, hugging and kissing him," he wrote and went on to suggest that their behavior was infantile and perhaps even less than manly. He felt that such conduct was certainly not good for the "image" of the sport. And so on. After reading the article, I laughed and wondered if this supercilious snob had ever been passionately involved in anything at all, not to understand the players' jubilation and uninhibited celebration of their teammate's goal. He probably

Elliot Denman, coach of the Shore A.C., helping Todd Scully gather himself after winning a tough race.

stopped kissing his parents after he was 12 or 13. I dismissed his views, feeling that since he hadn't gone through it, he just couldn't understand it.

Yes, we were passionately involved. Yes, we have embraced. Yes, we have kissed and hugged each other after our 2 mile relay team came from behind to grab first place. When Steve made the Olympic team, we were practically in tears with the joy of his accomplishment, knowing what motivation and deprivation and hard work went into it. When Roy hugged me for being there and helping when Ron won the NCAA cross-country title, it was a genuine and warm display of affection of one friend for another.

In 1946 DeWitt Clinton High School had the finest cross-country team it had ever had. It was as a part of that team that I was first exposed to team spirit. Regardless of race, religion or ability, I was a runner and was made to feel like a welcome addition to the team. I had a responsibility toward that team, and the team and its members had a responsibility toward me. We practiced together every day, going for most of the distance at whatever pace the slowest man could handle. Then at a certain point in the workout, we were each on our own and had to get back to the starting line as best we could. Staying with the slowest man was a lesson in encouragement, inspiration and teamwork. If we could inspire the slowest man to hang on and improve his performance, the team as a whole would finish closer together, improving chances for the team championship. You get to know just how much you can push someone and how much that person will push himself or herself. You gain respect for a person with guts, who can push past the pain.

Day after day, we trained together, sweated together, encouraged each other and laughed a lot. Then we rejoiced together in victory and wiped the brow of the man who threw up after a hard effort. Even the simple passing of the water bottle as we slaked our thirst together portrayed the sharing, respect and close communication that comrades have with each other. Is it any different on the battlefield? Or at a construction site? It was no different at N.Y.U., the Pioneer Club or at the Long Island A.C.

Steve Hayden, '72 Olympian, now retired from racewalking, on our team:

Looking back on my years as a Long Island A.C. racewalker reminds me how lucky I was to be part of a close group of people. Our original group included five guys all dedicated to training together on weekends and many times after work. Training never became a bore; it was a real social experience we all looked forward to. We became such close friends through our common goals that the camaraderie we built was a part of my life I now miss.

Memories we cherish. Long Island A.C. Teammates, June 1960. *Top* Gary Westerfield, Howie Jacobson, Steve Hayden. *Bottom:* Larry Newman, John Markon.

But the closeness went beyond runners and running or walkers and walking. Our sport was only the *thing* that brought us together. We were not just runners or walkers. We were people with a common interest, who spent hours at a time with each other. Because of traffic, we broke off in pairs and spent most of the workout discussing anything from gardening to physics to job possibilities to family, or to John's and my liking for baroque music. We had an opportunity to discover each other as people and found that some of us were quite multifaceted individuals.

Our group of highly motivated and highly individual athletes became a social group, interacting with each other and opening up to each other and finding that, aside from the admiration and respect for each other as runners or racewalkers, we really liked and related to each other on so many levels. We enjoyed each other so much that we began to socialize at night or on weekends. We "ran around" together as students and "walked around" and partied together also as couples. We have seen marriages, divorces, births, deaths, good times and bad times—still friends.

In this highly mobile society in which we live, many of us have relocated to different parts of the country, but the warm friendships started through our associations with running and racewalking will endure for a lifetime. I cherish our times together and I know they feel the same.

15

HAZARDS
Birds, Bees, Dogs, Cars, Bikes, Heat, Cold

We put in so many miles training and racing, day after day, year after year. Most of it is solid, self-reflective time which also may even be boring at times. I must admit, however, that for me, in my 35 years, I rarely ever felt bored. I always enjoyed and looked forward to training and racing. There have been occasions, in fact, when it was quite exciting—and sometimes downright scary. That was when Mother Nature and the elements came into play, and sometimes man was playing too in a mean, if not vicious, manner. As I reflect on some of those times now, I cannot help but be philosophical. Something almost invariably so good has to have a few bad features. Like the time I began being very wary of birds. My first experience with an aggressive bird was in 1967 at 6 A.M. in Westbury, Long Island. I was out for my morning 6 mile workout on a tree- and shrub-lined road with not too much traffic at that hour of the morning.

At the 5 mile mark, a pigeon suddenly swooped up in front of me about 30 feet in the air, arced behind me to head level about 20 feet behind, and then headed right for me. I ducked, waved my hand and looked up as it made another arc. Again at the level of my head it came at me. I pulled out my spray can and squirted a stream at it. The pigeon flashed away and made still another arc. I had been walking but now started running. That pigeon kept following me. I threw gravel or rocks at it every time it made a pass at me. I got to the corner gas station, went inside and looked up at it, waiting for me on the telephone wire. I went outside and ran to my street. The pigeon lighted on the Stop sign. Throwing a rock at it, I ran into my house, shaken by this crazy experience. When I went to work an hour later it was gone. Later that morning I called the Audubon Society who told me that I must have disturbed its nest. For a few mornings afterward, I was really nervous as I remembered Hitchcock's movie, *The Birds*.

All these years have passed and there have been no more similar incidents, nor had I heard of any, until I took a beach house on Fire Island.

One gray overcast morning I was training along the beach road at Robert Moses State Park. And from the very beginning of my work-out to the 3 mile turnaround and back again was like running a gauntlet. Every 40 or 50 yards another small blackbird would swoop down on me and harass me. Never in pairs and never actually pecking me, but each one, as I learned later, was trying to establish its own territoriality. I told my teammate and protégé, Peter Timmons, who occasionally works out with me on that same road. He laughed and found it incredible because we were never attacked when we walked together. However, a couple of weeks later on a day when I didn't show up for a workout, he became a believer. The birds harassed him!

Dan O'Connor, one of America's best young racewalkers, lived in the Dominican Republic for 2 years. He told me of some of his experiences with small birds, hawks and falcons. He told about giant bats with a wingspan of up to 3 feet, swooping around and just missing, never actually touching him. He also told me about the tarantula spiders that jumped 3 to 5 feet in the air to get out of his way as he walked down the road—training in the interior jungle forest.

On each course where we work out, we always check for a favorite pit stop. One sunny Saturday morning we were training in the Westbury Hills of Long Island. I felt the urge but couldn't wait to get to our arboreal bathroom, so I ducked into some bushes adjacent to a pasture. My teammates thought I was crazy when I came crashing out of there yelling, smacking my own behind and waving my arms frantically. I had practically squatted on a swarm of bees! You had also better check out the bushes you duck into because Larry Newman got a bad case of poison ivy after a visit to a pit stop.

Westbury, Long Island, is a fairly affluent community with many large homes and estates. There are some wonderful courses laid out, with really beautiful scenery. As in many other suburban areas, there are lots of dogs who are anxious to protect their own territory. And they were our biggest problem. We got to know which houses or driveways had which dogs, how friendly or mean they were, and how we could handle getting by them without having a chunk bitten out of our hides.

Scram, you guys! This is *my* turf.   *Wide World Photos*

First of all, we never showed a dog that we were afraid of him, for that would encourage him. We still laugh today about our esteemed colleague, who shall remain nameless, hiding behind us when we were threatened by a dog. One corner property had two very big dogs. One day one of them came charging out on the road, surprising us. We had no stones, no sticks—nothing. I took one step forward and gave the charging dog an uppercut punch. Then we all started flailing our fists at it until he retreated. From then on, we picked up sticks and carried them past that property. Whenever we passed the Reverend Spencer's house, his mouse of a dog would come scampering down to the side of the road, barking shrilly. All we had to do was look at her, and she would turn and run back to the house. Farther down the road lived a big German shepherd—we just walked on the other side of the road to avoid him. One day we were surprised and extremely scared when a big, vicious-looking black Labrador retriever came crashing out from the bushes without warning. Much to our relief he was just a friendly jogger. He accompanied us then and on other occasions for a couple of miles at a time. My friend, Katalin, told me that the same thing happened to her near her summer house in Rhinebeck, New York. Her dog sometimes followed for 10–15 miles.

Our climate in the East can go from one extreme to the other. In summer it can reach 100°F and in winter drop as low as 5°F below zero. But for the most part, it is not too uncomfortable. In extreme weather, however, there are dangers such as heat exhaustion and heatstroke, or hypothermia and frostbite.

Heat exhaustion occurs when the body loses large amounts of water and electrolytes—sodium, magnesium, potassium—through perspiration during prolonged exercise. It is accompanied by fatigue, nausea and headache. Sufferers usually remain conscious and have a rapid pulse of 100–140 beats per minute with rectal temperature elevated to 102° to 104°F. The skin continues to sweat but is pale and clammy. Treat heat exhaustion by removing the person to the shade and give him or her plenty of fluid and rest.

Heatstroke may not be far behind. There is no sweating and the skin is red and hot. The person may become delirious and then unconscious. The pulse goes up to 120–160 beats per minute. The rectal temperature may be as high as 105° to 106°F. The treatment for heatstroke is more dramatic and speed in reducing temperature is vital. Cool the person off immediately. Pull him into a shaded or cool area. Place him in shock position with the feet up and the head down. Soak him in wet sheets or towels or immerse him in a cool bath, if possible, in order to start heat evaporation through the skin. Rub ice all over the body. When he regains consciousness, give him cool liquids. Get him to a hospital fast, particularly if he cannot communicate intelligibly.

The key to efficient performance in hot weather training and racing is water. You must keep your fluid level up so that it keeps your blood volume normal. So drink plenty of liquids before you work out (10–12 ounces) and plenty (a similar amount each ½ hour) during the workout. During a long distance race on a hot day, you can lose 8 to

10 pounds of fluid. A walker can dehydrate twice as fast as he or she can replace the fluids during a race. There are specially prepared drinks that help to replace the electrolytes lost during exercise. They all have some good qualities, but I prefer orange juice, tomato juice and plain water. Water should be the most often used replacement Also pour it over your head and your body on a particularly hot day.

Olympian Tom Dooley snatches a drink on his way to winning the 1967 National 40 km Championship at Long Beach, New Jersey. *Asbury Park Press photo by Herman Gerechoff*

A temperature reading of 75°F will be 10° higher in direct sun and if it is also humid—watch out. In humid weather it is difficult for the sweat you produce to evaporate and cool the body. Try to make up for it by drinking more and splashing cold water on yourself. As Dr. Sheehan says, "Water saves, heat can kill."

The other extreme—cold—can also be dangerous, and even deadly. Frostbite is freezing damage to the skin and underlying tissues, usually from direct exposure to extreme cold. The fluid between the cells freezes, and the cells themselves are cut off from nutrients. Occasionally, the tissue involved dies, and the damage is so severe that, in the case of a finger, it may have to be amputated to prevent gangrene. Recognizing frostbite is not too difficult. There is a feeling of severe cold and pain in the exposed part. These are usually the fingers, toes, ears, nose or the cheeks. A burning sensation follows and the affected part takes on a whitish color. Don't rub it! You can cause severe tissue damage or infection. The frozen tissue must be rewarmed rapidly. The best way is to place it in warm water (no hotter than 107°F), or if warm water is unavailable and it can be done physically, tuck it between the thighs or under the armpits. If that is impossible, cover the affected part well, and if within 20 minutes of the emergency treatment normal color and sensation don't return, get to a doctor.

Hypothermia occurs when the body's internal "core" temperature drops 10–20 degrees. This can occur even when the outside temperature is no colder than 30–50°F, more often because the person has become wet and remained in the cold. Heat can be lost quite rapidly by the body. I have seen many athletes remain in clothing wet with perspiration after training or racing, only to begin shivering shortly thereafter. The clothing has begun to dry, and the evaporation process causes cooling of the skin, which produces shivering. Shivering is an involuntary contraction of the muscles to generate heat and is usually the first signal that the core temperature has begun to drop. Get indoors and strip off the wet clothing immediately. If I had to remain for the awards presentation after a race, I used to strip off my wet turtleneck and T-shirt, and put on my outer sweatshirt or jacket, next to my skin—a trick that I learned years ago. Most of the time these days, I rub myself with a coarse, dry towel and put on a dry sweater from my bag. Warm liquids and some food, preferably quick-energy sugars, should be next. If it is a mild lowering of temperature, then a warm bath, along with warm drinks and plenty of blankets should suffice. If the fever thermometer fails to rise above 94°F, then call the doctor. Hypothermia can be fatal if not treated immediately.

Winter racing (and training) can be fun, but learn how to stay warm. *Asbury Park Press photo by Herman Gerechoff*

If Mother Nature is sometimes bad, human nature is sometimes worse. You never have any trouble or remarks from athletes, only from idiots in cars or on bikes or the nonathletic morons who listen to their loud portable radios and snicker and sneer and make comments at anyone and everyone doing something for his body.

As I was training on the bicycle path in lower Central Park, I approached a young couple, strolling along toward me. The rather fat young man said, "I used to walk like that until my doctor cured me." She laughed until I answered, "You should have asked him to cure your fat body," as I passed them. Neither smiled and there was no retort.

I get all kinds of whistles and comments, most of which can be ignored. Occasionally, when some people have yelled out, "Hey, that's cheating, that's not jogging," I answer, "No, it's racewalking, and it's better." The most fun I get is when one youth will yell out from a group, "Shake your boodie," or "Move it, honey." I stop and smile and ask if anyone wants to race. Here's what happened the last time I made the offer:

"Yeah man, I'll race yuh. Yeah, we'll race."

"O.K. But you have to walk." (And I explained the rules.) "Ready. Go!" And I took off, leaving them struggling far behind.

Then I feel good because the comments always change to: "Right on, man." "Way to go!" Another observation I have made about passersby who whistle or make remarks at racewalkers is that they never do or say anything if they are alone. There has to be at least two of them.

It has been said that when a person gets behind the wheel of a car, he has a different personality. I believe it. Some of my worst experiences have been with cars actually trying to run me down. One bright summer morning while I was training on the service road to the Long Island Expressway, an approaching car with six guys in it veered to run me off the road. As I always walk facing traffic and am always prepared for the worst, I dove for the side of the road, saw a rock, picked it up and in one motion rolled to my feet and threw the rock which hit and broke the rear side window. The car screeched to a halt. From a racewalker I became a sprinter and ran like hell, climbed the fence onto the Expressway and put plenty of distance between us. I may have retreated, but I think I won both the battle and the war.

Another time on a street adjacent to the Northern State Parkway, a man in a car behind me came up to within 5 feet of me and "sat" on his horn. I was walking south, 6 inches from the curb, taking the only course available on that road, so that for a couple of blocks, I had to walk in the direction of traffic. The horn really startled me (I was deep in meditation) and made me angry. Two men were in the front seat enjoying a good laugh at my expense. I gave them the middle finger, shouted two choice words, and went on to the sidewalk until Oyster Bay Road, crossed it and turned north, walking on the left side of the road facing traffic. Suddenly, an approaching car tried to run me down. I jumped left behind a stout tree on the sidewalk. It was those same two guys! After missing me, they made a screeching "U" turn and came back past me. I started to smile while tossing a fist-sized rock from one hand to the other. Upon seeing the rock, they kept on going. I had made my point.

Training in Westbury, we've had soda and beer cans tossed at us; we've been bombed with dirt clods from a landscaper's truck; and we've been spat at. Once in Long Branch, New Jersey, I got half a can of beer in my face. People in cars. Watch out for some of them. They are *crazy*.

Serious, competitive bike riders are O.K. They understand training and dedication. But some of the clowns who zip around with big radios slung on their bikes have similar mentalities to the car-driving maniacs. They don't ride in the fixed lanes for cyclists, nor do they go in the prescribed direction, despite warnings by the park bike patrol. In one month one of my East Side Track Club racewalkers was hit twice, once head-on and once from behind.

During my very first racewalk in Central Park more than 20 years ago, a biker approaching me veered right at me to make me jump out of the way. I didn't see him, being so intent on my race. At the last moment I spotted him, made a stiff arm and fist, caught him on the side of the jaw, and sent him sprawling. People around us laughed when he looked up and asked, "What did you do that for?" (They had seen what had happened.) Me? I just kept going.

Regular racewalkers encounter such things from time to time, but I've not told you these episodes to discourage you. Not at all. Some people feel they have to do their thing even if it's mean or insane. They are not so many or so fearsome that they can make *us* not do *our* thing. And forewarned is forearmed.

16

CHILD'S PLAY
The Younger the Better

Children. They are so beautiful and so natural. Like little animals they play, run, touch and sniff with infinite curiosity. We love them, guide them, chide them and try to show them how to fend for themselves. For the most part we do a good job of it. But I think that we could do a better job.

The average suburban housewife and mother drives her children to little league, girl scouts, boy scouts, Sunday school, regular school, music lessons and on and on. She is always uptight about it, feeling pressured because she has to do it, guilty if she doesn't always do it. I realize that there are some other factors involved. We raised four children in the suburbs. If the distances are just too far, the child too young, the weather too inclement, O.K., do it. But also realize that we tend to spoil our children. We *could* encourage them to bike it, or walk it, or run it much more than we allow them to do. Why? Because in many cases, we overprotect them. We worry too much. They can handle the distance. We, as a nation, are underexercised, and it begins with the children. They are overfed and underexercised. We worry that they don't eat enough, and we reward them with junk foods and soft drinks and sweets.

A fat baby is not necessarily a healthy baby. Some chubby children never shed their "baby fat." The obese teenager is not going through a "stage," automatically becoming slim and trim as an adult. The children of obese parents who have heart conditions, hypertension

222

and other disorders, are more likely to develop these same problems themselves. The answer to childhood obesity is to nip it in the bud with early supervision of diet and exercise. My oldest boy was put on a diet at 6 months of age because he was too fat. Cutting the caloric intake of a fat child and encouraging him to exercise and play games with other children will create a negative energy balance. Many fat children become even fatter because they hide behind their fat. They feel inadequate to the other children when it comes to athletic games, so they stay home and eat.

The best thing to do is to encourage your children to go for a walk with you. Now, I am not going to be fanatic and say that you should all have your children involved in racewalking and make competitors out of them. If for some reason they can't run and play, then you'd do well to spend some time with them walking and talking, rather than watching that football or baseball game—or soap opera.

Nine-year-old Diana Romansky, daughter of Olympian and National Champion Racewalker Dave Romansky, displaying excellent style at the annual Boardwalk Ten Mile, Asbury Park, New Jersey. *Andy Novick*

Dr. George Sheehan called the 9-year-old child "pound for pound the world's best endurance athlete. The nearest thing to perpetual motion in human form you will ever see." The 9-year-old, according to physiological studies, has the greatest heart volume for his weight that he will ever have, unless he turns into a champion runner or racewalker.

Many children have high rates of oxygen uptake, showing good aerobic fitness. There are some 9- and 10-year-old children who have higher oxygen uptake volume than many highly trained runners and racewalkers.

Where do these children get a chance to display this awesome amount of energy and precocious ability? Oddly enough, it is not in our schools. A few years ago Dr. Paul Dudley White, the world-renowned cardiologist, wrote expressing his medical view for proper physical education in the schools:

> I find that a gross error is now being made in various places to reduce or even omit compulsory physical education. There is a rush to stuff the brains of our youths with information that they may never utilize to the full because of the probability of early death or disability originating from their lack of physical fitness. It is a sad commentary on the defects of our current education that the sons of our patients . . . are developing cardio-vascular disability much earlier in life—as shown, for example, by an onset of angina pectoris at an age of 13 years younger than in the case of the fathers.

At the high school and college level, the community and the parents are so strongly interested in spectator sports that in most of our communities, good facilities and coaching are provided only for "varsity" athletics. This is the group that needs them the least—those who are already physically fit and talented. Unfortunately, the community is likely to think that having successful teams means having a sound physical education program.

As a result of that distorted thinking, the majority of the students are neglected. Not enough emphasis is placed on non-team sports and exercise programs that the individual can learn, participate in and enjoy on a lifetime basis. The teaching process for physical fitness should begin earlier, explaining why it is important to be fit and how to stay fit. More background information and theory should be taught so that children can understand *why* they are doing various exercises. More should be taught about proper diet, and nutritional lunches should be served in the cafeterias. Some schools are *proud* of the fact that they have introduced fast-food lunches that are very popular with the children. Do they care about how much cholesterol and fat those foods have? We are feeding obesity and heart disease!

I expect that about now, many of you are waiting for my fervent pitch for racewalking in the schools. Well, I hope that I will fool you. I am not such a zealous proselytizer for racewalking that I am blind to other sports. Let children play. It's too early for specialization. They should be exposed to *all* sports. Children should be able to run and jump, climb and play. They should know what it is to win and to lose. They should learn how to get along and play with other boys and girls. The more exposure the better. Noncontact sports in a non-competitive or low-key competitive situation is a great outlet for the abundance of energy that children have, as well as teaching them motor skills and eye–hand coordination. The formative years are most important as the bones and surrounding muscles, tendons and ligaments will grow and set. Improper placement and alignment will set them wrong.

"The younger the better," says Henry Laskau, shown here teaching his son, Howard, to racewalk.

Now, here comes my pitch for racewalking *especially* for children. I emphasize, however, that I recommend exposure to racewalking only in conjunction with running, jumping, throwing and other team and individual sports.

Why racewalking? Because if proper walking style is learned early, then many of the foot, leg, hip and lower back problems that children and adults acquire as a result of improper style can be avoided. Through racewalking young people will learn to walk with proper alignment, thereby allowing the muscle-tendon units in the feet and legs to grow and strengthen properly without undue stress. The race-walking style will teach them to coordinate their arm and leg movements, help to build their upper bodies, and enable them to walk with power, fluidity and grace. Just acquaint them with it. That is all that I ask.

Nine-year-old Carrie Foote of New York City, and Fran Kerse of New Zealand stepping out at the annual Mother's Day 10 km in Central Park. Note Carrie's excellent foot placement and vigorous arm swing.

Some youngsters are more self-directed than others, are more competitive at an early age, and have developed a keen interest in a specific sport. Little league baseball and soccer, gymnastic clubs, swimming clubs, the Road Runners Club of America, and the Walkers Club of America, among others, have given youngsters age 6 to 16 an opportunity to be exposed to sports and qualified coaching that they do not get at the elementary school level.

Despite the criticism leveled at the little league baseball system because of interfering parents and overpushy coaches, it does offer most youngsters good experiences in team play. And please credit the coaches and managers. They are volunteers and well-meaning, you know.

One of the biggest growth areas has been in European football, or soccer as we call it in this country. Leagues are set up, giving both boys and girls an opportunity to develop their ability, strength and speed. Television coverage of Olympic and international competitions has given a tremendous boost to public interest in gymnastics. Youngsters everywhere are seeking to emulate Olga Korbut, Nadia Comaneci and Kurt Thomas. Swimming has been far ahead of other sports in discovering that champions can be developed at a very early age. The Europeans have been ahead of us in this regard. We Americans have just begun to test this application in sports other than swimming. We should have learned a lesson from ballet dancers, who begin very early in life to train their bodies.

The Road Runners Club of America has had one of the most successful age-group programs in athletics. The national age-group chairman, Barry Geisler, has done a fantastic job of promoting running for children.

Nine-year-old Noah Gelber, striding beautifully at a racewalking clinic co-sponsored by the New York Road Runners Club and the New York Walkers Club in Central Park, New York City.

The Walkers Club of America has always had separate prizes for children competing in various races. Diana Romansky (shown earlier) and her sister Denise, age 15, have been setting various age-group records for the past few years. They happen to have a good coach. Developmental races—giving handicaps (headstarts based on time or distance) to slower walkers—keeps them encouraged and interested in the sport. Free racewalking clinics are given by many of the local chapters.

The net result of the club function in the various sports mentioned before has been to foster interest and develop talented youngsters who continue to do well at the high school and college level. In the clubs everyone plays, everyone competes. The competitive spirit promotes healthy growth and achievement.

Let them play. Let them participate and compete—win or lose. Let it be fun. Encourage them but don't push them. Praise the youngster who wins and be supportive of the loser. Don't try to laugh off a poor showing. Expose children to many different sports, but competition is not for everyone. If your school district is not doing a good job of introducing your children to sports in which they can participate for a lifetime, then you do it. Help them to become athletes to whatever their degree of competence. Set an example for them. An apple doesn't fall very far from the tree.

17

THE WOMAN ATHLETE
Racewalking Is Better for You

Sweat. Nice, wet, salty sweat. It's the result of honest, hard work. It's no longer called perspiration and daubed away daintily with a lace handkerchief. It's what you have to work up if you want to trim or firm your figure. It's what you have to experience in order to participate or compete well in a sport. They are even giving out college scholarships if you do it well enough. Sports such as track and field, gymnastics, basketball, tennis and swimming are now part of comprehensive athletic programs for women in many of our colleges and universities today. And it's about time!

It's no surprise to look over a woman's shoulder on the train or bus and find her reading the sports pages. Newspaper and television coverage of the Olympic Games and international sporting events has fostered tremendous interest from women fans. Women's athletics have seen many great athletes over the years: Babe Didrikson, Gertrude Ederle, Fannie Blankers-Koen, Peggy Fleming, Wilma Rudolf, Billie Jean King, Donna DeVarona, Chris Evert, Olga Korbut, Nancy Lopez, Nadia Comaneci and Grete Waitz, to name just a few. And we ain't seen nothin' yet! It's only the tip of the iceberg. One day there will be women's racewalking and women's marathon in the Olympics. According to the Perrier study, "Women are getting involved in sports and athletics at a more rapid rate than men." While many women past their teens begin to exercise to improve their figures, many are realizing that certain athletic activities are fun and fulfilling—both the training and the competition. Many will never compete at all but are athletes nevertheless, and wouldn't miss a day of training.

For centuries, women were outside of that special group enjoying the camaraderie of athletics. Not participating in sports or athletics to any great extent, they were unaware of those warm and special feelings that training and friendly competition engender. Many friendships are started through involvement in athletics. The fitness boom has given women exposure to values other than immediate physical improvement. Many women feel more relaxed and free from tension and anxieties after physical training. They also have greater self-esteem because of their training accomplishments. Many feel more equal to men physically when they discover they too can cover 5 or 10 miles in a workout.

If you will stand near the finish line of a race, you will see competitive spirits at a peak to beat out that person coming up to one's shoulder, with no respect for age or sex. We all have it, and women are no exception. Whether it be in business or athletics, women are in the race. They're getting better and better at it and enjoying it all the more.

As for the trimming and slimming, many women desire to lose weight or keep from gaining it. Others want to firm up to prevent "middle-aged spread." Well, worry no more. Racewalking will do it all for you—more safely and firmly.

Now, if you want to avoid that "spread" you can literally *walk* your behind off. You can do the same thing for your thighs and stomach, too. A word here about cellulite is appropriate. Dr. David Costill, Director of the Human Performance Laboratory at Ball State University in Indiana, says, "Cellulite is anatomically speaking— fat." Any dimpling is caused by an uneven distribution—both in size and amounts—of fat cells. The weight loss that you achieve from walking will be from all over your body. Whenever you use a muscle or muscle group, hormonal signals are sent to every fat cell in your body. These cells then release molecules of fat into the bloodstream, which carries them to the laboring muscles to be used as fuel. The Columbia University study showed that racewalking is a dynamic way to burn calories. So if you want to lose weight faster—racewalk.

Here is where the firmer part comes in: Because of the fact that the muscles in the fronts of the legs and the backs of the legs are working equally in racewalking, as opposed to running where the backs of the legs do most of the work and the fronts relatively little, the race-walker develops more evenly balanced, stronger legs. Stronger and firmer with more definition—a slimmer and firmer leg. The gluteus maximus, gluteus medius and gluteus minimus—the three buttock muscles—are only moderately active during normal walking but contract with appreciable intensity during racewalking. That makes race-walking *the* gluteus maximus minimizer!

A racewalker uses the upper torso and arms in a much more vigorous fashion than a jogger or a distance runner. The arm action of a racewalker is dynamic—like that of a sprinter. This powerful arm movement builds firm and strong muscles of the arms, chest, abdomen and back. Many women have excess fat on the backs of their upper arms. With a general weight loss and/or with racewalk training, a woman can firm and trim her upper arms. That goes for the spare tire around the middle as well.

Water retention is another problem that some women complain about. This, at times, causes a thickening around the ankles and lower legs. With proper diet and a racewalking program, this too can be controlled. Some of the women in my program have trimmed their legs wonderfully and gained beautiful and shapely definition of the calf muscles.

If you're in it because you want to "lose," you'll "win" with racewalking. You will use almost all of the muscles in your body while racewalking. You will burn off your excess fat, reshape your body, and firm your muscles. But you need not fear the myth that you will become a musclebound female athlete. Your hormonal balance will not be altered by your exercise. The female hormone, estrogen, works for you so that you won't build bulging muscles—only firm them. Your well-proportioned body can still be lean and lithe and attractive to all.

The subject of hormones brings us to a review of the biological functions involved in racewalking or in any endurance sport for that matter. Except for the reproductive function, there are no important biological differences between men and women that should affect performance. Witness that fact by the tremendous reduction of the elite women's marathon times as compared with the elite men's times. Women are fast catching up and are beginning to find out how far and fast they can push their bodies. The very same applies to women's performances in racewalking which, in the last two years, has become one of the fastest growing sports for women.

The decades of the 1960s and 1970s were times when women took off their bras, both literally and symbolically. The quest for equality has extended to athletics as well. It is a myth that special considerations must be made for the female racewalker because of her reproductive functions. The menstrual cycle will not interfere at all with racewalking. Premenstrual tension, leg swelling and pelvic cramps have been found to be alleviated by racewalking. A West Point study showed that women who regularly engage in vigorous physical activity have fewer menstrual complaints such as headache, fatigue and cramps. The flow may be heavier, but it will be less uncomfortable. Because of heavy blood loss, however, an iron supplement should be taken.

Amenorrhea, the absence of the menstrual period, occasionally seems to occur in athletes as opposed to nonathletes. Of the athletic group, those who train over 50 miles a week, as opposed to those who train only 20–25 miles, have a significantly higher incidence of amenorrhea. Many gynecologists and sportsmedicine specialists link this with the percentage of fat of a woman's total weight. In the average woman, body fat constitutes 20–25 percent. In women athletes it is more like 15–18 percent. But in racewalkers, distance runners and ballet dancers, it could drop to 12 percent or less. Whatever the reason for its occurrence, either from strenuous activity or from a lower percentage of body fat, there is no cause for alarm. Amenorrhea has no link to a long-term impairment of fertility. When heavy training ceases and a weight gain is experienced, the normal menstrual cycle returns.

Fat has another role in the body, that of storing energy. It would seem, therefore, that if someone had slightly higher fat reserves, he could perform better in distance walking than a person with less fat. But it doesn't work that way. There is a disadvantage in carrying around the extra weight. Speaking of extra weight, let's see what happens when a pregnant woman racewalks.

Racewalking is, in fact, a better exercise for the pregnant woman than running or jogging. Racewalking eliminates the jarring action of running. Instead, it offers a smooth transfer of weight. Because of the posture-building style of racewalking, there will be fewer back pains. Aching legs and varicose veins are avoided because of the "milking" action of the muscles and blood vessels of the legs during racewalking. Proper breathing and good posture, along with vigorous walking, will keep the abdominal muscles in good condition. Most obstetricians advocate physical exercise, at least during the first and second trimesters. Some prescribe it right up until term. Studies indicate that women athletes have easier and shorter deliveries and recover faster as a result of their better conditioning.

Bones, muscles, tendons and ligaments are biologically indistinguishable between the sexes. Yet the injury rate for women is much higher than for men. The highest rate of injury has been in running where, in the last 2 years, women's involvement in injuries has grown by 73 percent as compared to a 53 percent increase in men. There are three reasons for this high injury rate: First, most women have not had exposure to the musculoskeletal stresses of regular athletics early in life, allowing them to develop better stress acceptability and capa-

The oldest and the youngest athletes in a women's 2-mile race in Williamstown, Massachusets: Mrs. Esther Babbitt, 83, and Bepi Barry, 3.

bility. Second, considering that most people, not just women, have been on an extended vacation from any kind of physical activity, the musculoskeletal system needs conditioning to prepare for the stresses of strenuous exercises, especially running. Third, the wider, built-for-child-bearing-pelvis of women causes undue pressure on their legs, from the foot right up to the hip and the lower back, while running.

Steven Subotnick, the running foot doctor, says that a reason why women runners are more prone to certain injuries than men is because of their wider pelvis. He also says that a cause of overuse injuries might be running itself. "Running increases the angular deformity of the lower extremities." I say that if women have wider pelvises, and running may cause more injuries, then more women should be racewalking, which does not put such stress on the legs. Remember, racewalkers are virtually injury-free.

The female heart and lungs are slightly smaller than the male's, but otherwise the cardiorespiratory systems of men and women are identical. When we exercise we increase the demand by the muscles for oxygen. Our hearts pump faster, and more air is moved in and out of the lungs and into the bloodstream. This adaptation represents increased efficiency in delivering oxygen to those working muscles. Achieving this efficiency is called the cardiorespiratory training effect, and it is achieved by male and female alike. Therefore, the beneficial physiological effects on the cardiorespiratory systems of men and women are identical.

As a woman, you may be able to keep your capacity for exercising longer into life than a man. Studies indicate that a man's endurance capacity declines about 7 percent per decade while a woman's declines only 3 percent.

If you haven't exercised for a while, remember to start gradually and not do too much too soon. Some of us gain in cardiorespiratory fitness quicker than our musculoskeletal systems. When we are feeling good, we have a tendency to begin to push ourselves. You may get some aches and pains from sore muscles, but that soreness is only a sign that your muscles are responding positively to the stimulation of exercise. Be sure that you do a lot of stretching, and adhere to the preparation programs I have outlined for you.

I hope you are reassured that physically you have everything to gain (except weight) by racewalking. But how about the emotional part? How about the joy of racewalking?

Physical effort puts you in touch with your inner self. An understanding of that effort will help you to tune in on your body, perhaps for the first time. You will realize that the body is the mind and the mind is the body. Through this liaison, you can better realize your potential as a woman and as an athlete.

Here you are with your commitment—your body and mind at the ready—awaiting the moment when you *will* yourself to move. Walking slowly, you begin to stride easily, arms and legs synchronized beautifully. Your breathing blends in with your movements and becomes deeper. You feel the power of your own stride when you reach out with your heel, roll along your foot, and push straight back with your toes. Your arms are pumping, and you can feel the muscles working in your entire upper body. You begin to feel the tingle of sweat starting to rise from your skin. Breathing in the fresh air, you feel rhythmical and graceful. It feels good. It all feels so good. And you feel good about yourself. And that is the joy of racewalking!

The commitment to fitness is an experience in self-knowledge. You learn about yourself. You learn about your coordination and physical capacity and about the daily changes in your body. You discover your attitudes, feelings of achievement and willpower. If you are tuned into yourself, the reason for cutting short your warm-up or

Susan Liers (98), Island track Club, New York, winning the 1978 Women's National AAU 5,000 meter racewalk championship in California, with a time of 25:46:8. *Wide World Photos*

your workout becomes clearly apparent to you. Did your body really reach its limit, or did the psyche rebel? The truth will out. You have to answer only to you. You are not someone's wife or sweetheart or someone's mother. You are *you*. They are *your* tired legs, *your* pounding heart, *your* determination to tell you to go one more lap or 10 more minutes. *You* get the exhilaration from willing yourself through that last lap, feeling the very real and personal pleasure of the achievement.

The woman whose body has been strengthened and toned by regular racewalking communicates a self-esteem and confidence that remains unknown to the woman who has ignored her body. You not only feel good, you look good.

The woman who wants to racewalk competitively has not been overlooked in this chapter. You who are already into the sport are ahead of your sisters. You train together and race many times with men. I see no reason for singling you out for special training. You know where you are going. You know that the field is wide open for athletes who are willing to dedicate time and energy to their sport.

Those of you who are competitive-minded but not yet in it have only to train according to my programs, outlined earlier. And when you feel that you are ready, come on along. There is room for plenty more!

18

THE OLDER ATHLETE
No Need to Slow Down

Age is for the birds. You are as young as you feel, but too many people become old before their time. The trouble is that they stop moving their bodies at a very young age. To rest is to rust. Many people rust out before they wear out. They don't realize the human body was made to be used for a lifetime. Many people don't do any physical exercise once they are out of high school or college. That begins their degeneration toward becoming sedentary old men and women—many of them while still only in their late 20s and 30s. You often hear:

"What? Exercise at my age?"

"But I'm too old for that kind of stuff!"

"I can't exercise. I'm too old and too heavy."

You are never too old to exercise. Nor, if you choose to, are you too old to compete. Neither are you too old to become an athlete. All you have to do is exercise on a regular basis. Thank God for the President's Council on Physical Fitness and Sports. Thank God for the masters and veterans movements in athletics. C. Carson Conrad, Executive Director of the President's Council on Physical Fitness and Sports, states that during the last 4 years, physical fitness classes for senior citizens have started in nearly every major American city. "Casey" Conrad, who is 68, also conducts workshops on fitness for the elderly, with more than 150,000 volunteer leaders participating. They are training thousands of new senior citizen athletes.

About 10 years ago, the masters movement in track and field and distance running got under way, giving the opportunity to runners and field athletes 40 years and older to participate in various competitions and to be scored on an age-group basis. Bob Fine, a former New York Pioneer Club teammate of mine, was and still is a driving force behind the movement as National Amateur Athletic Union Masters Chairman. The Road Runners and the Walkers Club of America have given masters competitors prizes as a separate category for some years now.

Masters Champion Don Johnson, 62 years young, walks with Tanya McIntosh, 12 years young, at the Boardwalk Ten, Asbury Park, New Jersey, 1979.

The masters movement stands out as an example of how men and women can remain athletes from their 40s right up to their 80s. They train and compete against their peers, and have physiologically sound bodies comparable to those 20 to 30 years younger. But this elite group of athletes were not athletes all their lives. Doctor George Sheehan had been a runner at Manhattan College, gave it up after college, and at the age of 45 became an athlete all over again. Seventy-five-year-old Paul Fairbanks of Washington did not start endurance training until he was 63. Mrs. Eugenia Henn, mentioned earlier, became an athlete at 60. New York Walkers Club athlete Gwen Clark is 87.

You can begin training at any age and with a regular program, you *are* an athlete. *No,* you are *not* too far gone. Here is an example of Pritikin's doing it again: Eula Weaver, a Santa Monica grandmother, went on Nathan Pritikin's diet and exercise program at the age of 81. She had arthritis, high blood pressure and a failing heart. Her circulation was so poor that she always had to wear gloves, even in summer. When she started, she couldn't walk more than 30–40 yards without discomfort. As a result of the program, by 1978, at the age of 88, she walks and runs, goes to a gym three to four times a week, and has surmounted many of the old-age syndromes that plagued her before.

Dr. Audrey C. Haschemeyer, Professor of Biology at Hunter College, New York, tells of her mother, Mrs. Betty Veazie, age 72, who lives in Woods Hole, Massachusetts. She developed diabetes about 10 years ago and angina 3 years ago. In consultation with her doctor, Thomas Sweeney of Falmouth, Massachusetts, she was put on a special diet and walking program 2 years ago. "Mrs. Veazie's condition is much improved," states Dr. Sweeney, and he now puts all of his patients able to handle physical exercise on a vigorous walking program.

Various surveys have been taken determining just how much exercise adult Americans do on a regular basis. According to a survey taken for the President's Council, only 39 percent of Americans aged 60 and over exercise regularly. The favorite form of exercise for this age group is walking, which is practiced by 46 percent of the men and 33 percent of the women who do exercise. But some of these people are almost apologetic about walking as exercise. They shouldn't be. They should be proud that they are walking for their health. Hear it from a great athlete who should know. Leo Sjogren, national champion cross-country skier and member of the 1952 and 1956 United States Olympic Racewalking Team said, "Every step that I take is a deposit in the bank of health."

It is interesting that 75 percent of the total population now realizes that the most important types of exercise are those that strengthen the heart and improve blood circulation. Yet, those least informed about the relative values of various exercises are people aged 50 and over. A survey conducted by Louis Harris and Associates for Great Waters of France, producers of Perrier bottled water, notes: "People 50 or over are more likely than others to feel that 3 hours of golf per week is enough to be fit. Fifty percent of those 65 and over make the same claim about bowling." Actually, 3 hours of bowling, baseball or golf per week would have almost no effect at all on cardiovascular efficiency. "Casey" Conrad stated in a report for the U.S. Department of Health, Education and Welfare: "The extremely low level of physical fitness of United States adults is basically due to attitudes toward exercises and fitness of most older citizens." These attitudes are as follows:

1. They believe their need for exercise diminishes and eventually disappears as they grow older.
2. They vastly exaggerate the risks involved in vigorous exercise after middle age.
3. They overrate the benefits of light sporadic exercise.
4. They underrate their own abilities and capacities.

Most senior citizens feel they have little physical capability. This is simply not true as evidenced by performances in the various senior exercise classes and in masters competitions.

Obviously, improving the physical fitness level of more older persons is a problem of education and of motivation. Not only do we have to educate this sector of the general population, but I believe we should have more workshops and conferences for physicians, especially to teach them about racewalking. The Perrier study questioned which factors would be most likely to increase chances of involvement in athletic activity. Forty-three percent of the nonactive public stated that a physician's recommendation to exercise would be the strongest motivational force urging them to do it. However, another survey found that physicians told only one of every five adults to exercise, and then they tended to prescribe only mild exercise and gave only generalized instructions at that. Too many physicians make statements such as, "Take it easy," or "You're in great shape for your age." In fairness to some of the physicians who do prescribe exercise, the patients do not always follow the advice. And many conscientious physicians spend their lifetime becoming intellectually fit, but they neglect their own physical fitness in the same manner in which they themselves live—smoking, drinking and eating too much. They certainly don't set an example for their patients. If every doctor had a subscription to *The Physician and Sportsmedicine,* he would certainly be more informed about sports and physical exercise and how they affect his own patients.

Many adults did not have good physical education and athletic experiences when they were young and are therefore not well informed about the contributions that physical exercise and being fit can make to their personal health, performance and appearance. Too many adults learned only about team sports rather than lifetime sports. Many of the activities and sports practiced as children and young adults are dropped upon graduation.

There are some high schools and colleges that have instituted individual prescription programs emphasizing:

1. Why people should exercise.
2. What their own personal exercise needs are.
3. How they can exercise to meet those needs.

The students learn from textbooks, lectures and demonstrations about various forms of exercise that are suitable to their needs. Each student is taught how to perform various exercises properly so as to achieve the maximum benefit from them. It is amazing to see so many adults today who don't know how to do a sit-up, or how to run properly. Participation for a lifetime is the goal of the course. Due to their increased knowledge, many students have become concerned about the fitness of their parents and have encouraged them to start exercising.

At a 1977 White House Conference on Aging at the National Institutes of Health in Washington, D.C., E. R. Buskirk, Ph.D., of Pennsylvania State University said: "Man at any age, if he is reasonably healthy, can be physically conditioned. While we may not be masters of our destinies, we can affect the degradation of our bodies." And I would add that if we are physically fit, we can even affect some of our own destinies!

At that same conference, Per-Olof Åstrand, M.D., the noted Stockholm physiologist, reported that training can modify a decline in maximal oxygen consumption with age. Dr. Åstrand said that studies have shown that some people maintain their maximum heart rate into old age and do not necessarily have it decline with age, as previously believed.

I have worked with many older people in my programs and clinics and have seen vast improvement in their fitness levels. With aging we tend to lose a slight range of motion in certain joints. Tendons and ligaments become less elastic. Arthritis may have affected the joints.

Bones lose calcium and fracture easily. The skeletal muscles gradually lose strength. The cardiovascular system, not being exercised, loses some capacity for work. Most of these conditions can be reversed by exercise. Whether you are 25, 45 or 85, you can begin a

Martin Fitzgerald, age 91, about to be overtaken by Olympian Dave Romansky.

program and become relatively fit. Sedentary persons and older persons, because of the conditioning they have lost due to age or lack of exercise, need to be eased into physical activity more gradually than the young. Slow racewalking is a great exercise for easing people into an endurance-fitness program. *The slowest jog is still more difficult than a slow racewalk.* Many older people just cannot jog at all. Many people who begin running run incorrectly, with improper alignment. Adding the shock factor of running to the ankles, knees, hip joints and the lower back causes much discomfort to many new runners. Racewalking eliminates that jarring and provides a smooth transfer of weight from one leg to the other. Slow racewalking eases a person into fitness by gradual improvement of the cardiovascular and musculoskeletal systems.

Caution to anyone over 35: A stress test is a must!

Using the pulse rate method is a good idea for a sedentary older person. For cardiovascular safety, use a heartbeat of 200 minus the age rather than the 220 figure used by sports physicians for most people.

As that person becomes more accustomed to racewalking, a slightly faster pace should be achieved, or else the subject should walk farther, or both as he finds he can take it without undue stress. This will cause the body to adapt to the new plateau, whether it be a quickened pace or a longer distance. Constant progress may be achieved by continually increasing the intensity (pace) and the duration (distance) of the walk. Just be sure to remain at a new level for a couple of weeks at a time and increase to a new plateau only a little at a time.

Caution: If you experience pounding in your heart or a pain in the chest, nausea, extreme breathlessness or trembling, STOP at once. If such distress lasts for more than a few minutes, check with your doctor. Perhaps you have overdone it. Back off. Go more slowly and not as far.

In general, older athletes become more physically fit than their contemporaries in the general population. They show less accumulation of fat, more lean tissue, a lower resting blood pressure and a greater aerobic capacity.

Spry is a term applied especially to the elderly if they are active, fit and agile. But something else usually accompanies this person who is thought of as being spry. They are usually "full of life," with a zest, alertness and acuity that causes people to speak admiringly of them.

Why? Because the circulatory value of walking keeps their brains young. With disuse comes atrophy. Exercise has been shown to ward off senility, keeping people alert and perceptive. It is not for physical health alone that older people should walk. It should be for their heads as well—to have more fun out of life—moving, seeing, enjoying. Those who are retired or work part-time can plan their day to include a racewalk session, maybe to a different part of town, or along a path by the river, with camera in hand.

So you see, age is no barrier to enjoyment. You can be youthful and vigorous at any age. It is a matter of attitude—the athlete's attitude. Identify with the athlete. Share with the athlete. There is no reason why the young (if they really are) should have it all. Racewalk and get your share!

FOUR

Racewalking's World

19

ORGANIZING RACEWALKS AND POPULAR MARCHES

Where does it all start? How does it all happen? Who are these people who compete in the Olympics and win various championship races?

It all starts at the grass roots, just like any other sport. Like the little league system or the school and collegiate system, it starts in small towns and big-city districts. Various competitions qualify race-walkers to compete in the district championships, the regional championships and then the national championships, which many times are held concurrently as qualifying races for Olympic and Pan American trials and for various international events that our country attends.

Wherever there are racewalkers, you'll find them organizing and competing in their own races. Many of the meets are decided upon the spur of the moment and used as time trials. A group of walkers decide to hold a race and they call some friends to come down and do the timing. Someone who has had some experience is called in to judge. Wives, children and friends will pass out refreshments. With or without prizes, you have the makings of a race. If the course has been measured, even on an automobile odometer (preferably two to check accuracy), then you're in business. It's loose, informal and fun. Many times we've held picnics right afterward.

If there is no Walkers Club chapter in your area, you can approach the local Road Runners Club about including a racewalking section in their upcoming races. The New York Road Runners Club has been

Ron Daniel, All-American Racewalker and National Champion, leading the pack in the Annual East side Track Club 10 km in Central Park, New York City, 1978. (Author Howard Jacobson is 514)

most cooperative in this regard. After all, it is a foot race, and no extra effort would be required. If you cooperate with them in some of their projects, I am sure they will welcome you into their races.

When it comes to staging a racewalk of some sizable dimension, like fifty or more racewalkers, then you must have more of an organization. The East Side Track Club has developed a format for staging road races. That, even with hand timing, can accommodate up to 300 racewalkers. Depending upon the size of your group, planning to stage a race will determine if one person will have to handle more than one job function. Most groups initially function with each person doing a number of jobs during the planning and preparation stage, and the groups gets more people to come in and help on race day. The key to staging a successful race is in the early planning. Put all of the job functions down on paper. Then follow through. Here are the various requirements for staging a race:

Planning and Preparation

- Pick a date that won't conflict with other races in your area or adjacent areas so that you will have a chance at maximum participation and attendance.

- Sponsors:
    local Chamber of Commerce
    YMCA, Police Athletic League, other organizations
    Department of Parks and Recreation
    businesses and corporations
- Find a site for the race:
    a school or campus
    a park
    road, streets
    shopping center
- Secure check-in, dressing facilities and toilet facilities, post-race award area.
- Obtain necessary permits:
    AAU (unless closed to club members only)
    parks department (if using the park)
    school authorities (if using a school or campus)
    police department (if traffic control is necessary)
    highways department (if you are using the roads)
- Remember to let the authorities know which official cars *you* will be using.

After seeing to the previous requirements, you can arrange for the rest:

- Decide the awards to be given and obtain them.
- Printing:
    posters
    entry forms
- Even though you have a release form on your entry blank, it may still be a good idea to obtain race-day liability insurance.
- Publicity:
    photographer
    press releases and pictures in advance
    results and pictures after race
    banners for race day
- Processing of advanced entries:
    preassigned numbers
    name and number to master control sheet
- Decide who will shoot the starter's gun. Many times obtaining a politician will insure your getting publicity and a picture in the press.

- Arrange for your timers.
- Measure course.
- Procure supplies:
  competitors' numbers
  safety pins
  numbered place tickets
  colored tape for start and finish (on ground)
  wool or string for first finisher
  clipboards
  pencils, pens
  colored ribbon for finish line chute
  starter's gun
  extra stopwatches
  bullhorn
  chief judge's flags, 1 white, 1 red
  preprinted forms for times, places
- Arrange for refreshments:
  water stations during race
  post-race sodas, bottled water, beer (You may get donations from a local bottling company or supermarket, or you may have to purchase.)
- Medical arrangements:
  doctor(s)
  podiatrist(s)
  extra volunteers
  tent, cots, blankets
  necessary equipment
  ambulance
- Make your calls to have plenty of volunteers (wives, children, friends); list them and call them the day before to remind them to report for a meeting just before the race. Preassign them beforehand and verify according to who shows up. Keep a few supernumeraries in abeyance for last-minute assignments.
- Remind your starter's office a couple of days before the event.

And Now the Race-Day

- Meeting of the various coordinators.
- Course clearly marked (possibly the night before), including mile markings.

No, you don't postpone races because of bad weather.

- Map(s) of course posted (unless on entry blank).
- Set up check-in table(s) for preassigned numbers.
- Set up registration table for post entries. Don't refuse them. We need all the walkers we can get.
- Meet with:
    judges
    timers—assign recorders to them
    number readers—assign recorders to them
    assigned person to give out place tickets
    police officer in charge
- Set up the medical unit.
- Press liaison/P.R. person to handle press and photographers.
- Set up concession sales if your club has T-shirts, patches, etc. and information table. Also make available entry blanks for upcoming races for your and other organizations.
- Set up water station(s).
- Timers, judges and officials to starting line.
Starting instructions
- Send volunteers to confusing turns on course to direct traffic.
- Arrange for intermediate times.
- Start the race: official car or police to lead the way.

- Finish line people in place:
    tape ready
    timers, recorders
    number readers, recorders
    giver of place tickets
- Stop watches when the first place finisher comes across the line. His time must be accurate for record purposes.
- Have a car follow the last place person.
- Judges' report.
- Room or table to tabulate results. Previously arranged chart listing various categories to receive awards will help speed tabulating.
- Set up refreshment table (during race).
- Set up awards table (during race).
- Cleanup crew for water stations, start and finish lines, and other areas used. Ask for cooperation of all.

The Award Ceremony

- Thank officials, police, volunteers, participants, sponsors.
- Results of race to newspapers.
- Within a week, send thank-you letters to sponsors, police, officials, volunteers.

Racewalks on a 440 yard or 400 meter track can be held for any distance, but they become unwieldy if you have more than twenty-five or thirty competitors. However, since world records are officially recognized only when raced on a track, there are a number of races contested on them. This requires strict attention to the counting of laps and giving the athletes their lap times. A mistake on the time is bad, but there is nothing that athletes hate more than someone's messing up their lap counting. It can cause them to go an extra lap or, even worse, be told later that they went one lap too few. I have seen athletes who normally are calm and soft-spoken individuals fly into an intense rage when a mistake is made on lap counting. Do you want to know something? I think that they are right. All their time and all the miles put into training screwed up by a careless mistake. It doesn't have to happen if you use a chart and provide a timer and a recorder team to keep the chart. The best paper to use is the back of a poster, 24 inches x 36 inches. Use two or four of them depending on how many competitors you have. You can even use 8½ x 14-inch sheets of paper if you don't have large poster paper. List the names and competitors' numbers down the left-hand margin and the mileage by laps across the top of the page. Use 1-inch spaces vertically for the names and 2-inch spaces horizontally for the miles with ½ inches for the lap times as shown:

Name	¼	½	¾	1	¼	½	¾	2	¼	½	¾	3
Young 1	1:51	4:01	6:00	8:01	10:00	11:58	14:00	16:00	18:01	20:01	21:59	24:02
Kitchen 2	2:00	4:01	6:00	8:02	10:01	11:59	14:00	16:01	18:01	20:01	22:00	24:02

The chart will work for 1 or 2 hour walks as well. Just don't have more competitors than can be accommodated by one team. A whole new group of competitors could be handled by another team. For example, women could be scored separately.

You might have to provide a chemical toilet for a long track walk so that the participants don't have to leave the track area.

The competitors' refreshment table should be set up *after* and away from the timing and scoring area. Otherwise, there is too much confusion. In strict races the helpers are not allowed to *hand* anything to the contestants. The drinks or fruit or whatever must be picked up from the table by the contestant. Labeled cups and bottles help in identification. Track walks, in my opinion, provide a welcome change from the road because you can develop more consistency by knocking off paced quarter-miles. You always know where your competition is and whether they are faltering or gaining. It is also good for judges and spectators because they can see you all the time.

People marches, or folk walks as they are sometimes called, are non-racing events held mostly in Europe and Israel. An annual 4-day walking event in Nijmegen, Holland, has been held since 1909. Attracting as many as 20,000 participants from many different countries, walkers must cover 30 to 50 kilometers per day, depending on age and sex. They don't walk for speed, only to participate and demonstrate fitness. Holland is truly a nation of walkers, with more than 500,000 ''event'' walkers. In 1969 I participated in the annual Jerusalem 3-day march which is patterned after the Nijmegen event. As in Nijmegen, prizes are awarded to teams in special categories, such as best precision marching by a corporation team, and so forth. It is quite a festival. Various groups and individuals register and receive accommodations in a tent city. At night there are pageants and folk dancing and an all-around good time. At a specified time in the morning, the group is scheduled to depart for the first day's march. There is nothing much to the organization. The advance publicity is what is more important. When people arrive at the site, they register, pay their entry fee, and receive assignments for billeting and meals (if it is more than a 1-day event) and the time their group is scheduled to depart from the starting line (so as to avoid crowds and confusion). All entrants receive a ribbon or a medal commemorating the event.

I hooked up with my friend, Shaul Ladany, with whom I had participated in "event" walks all over Israel. We went up to the front of the line to meet a few other walkers with whom we would race the distance. It was still dark when the starting cannon boomed, and we took off. Each day we walked via a different route.

Walking through tiny Arab villages on narrow winding paths with small houses, olive trees, and goats bleating beyond the piled stone walls made me feel as if I were back in Biblical times. No cars, no television, no electricity, no running water—and there I was, racing by in track shoes, shorts and a singlet! I sometimes wonder who is better off: we with our gasoline shortages, inflation and rush-rush civilization or they for whom time seems to have stood still, primitive but seemingly peaceful and content. They carry their burdens *on* their heads. We carry our burdens *in* our heads.

Shaul and I walked together and finished together during the first 2 days. We would get back to the practically deserted camp and have the comfort of taking a leisurely shower, eating and lying around in the sun, reminiscing about our racewalking experiences back in the States. Toward the middle of the afternoon, the camp would come alive when the quite tired but still singing and laughing groups started to filter back from their trek. Then came another night of campfires with singing, dancing and brotherhood.

The last day we were scheduled to walk 50 kilometers directly into Jerusalem. Shaul had to attend to some business in the city so I accompanied him to the gates of the city. We had been through some of the most picturesque and beautiful countryside filled with stirring history. I was so uplifted by what I saw and by where I had been that I turned around and went back 25 kilometers to see part of it again. On the way there and back, while passing the participants, many

PROFILE OF A CHAMPION
Neal Pyke

Neal Pyke leading the way in the
National Sports Festival 20 km Racewalk.
United Press International

An overnight sensation, that's Neal Pyke, who in March of 1976 first attempted racewalking by doing a mile in 8:36. Six weeks later he qualified for the Olympic Trials. He didn't make the '76 Olympic Team, but he sure has made a tremendous impact on American racewalking ever since.

Born in Mechanicsburg, Pennsylvania, in 1948, he is 6 feet tall and weighs 145 pounds. Neal was graduated from the University of Florida in 1975 and now resides in Belmont, California. In 1977 he made the indoor United States Track Team, competing in Toronto, Canada, against Canada and the U.S.S.R. He also made the summer team and set a new American record of 42:22 for 10 kilometers against the West Germans, and in Sochi, U.S.S.R., became the first American ever to win against the Russians when he won the 20 km road race. He also won the National AAU 15 km Championship and was part of the United States team for the World Team Championships. Not bad after racewalking only 1 year! In 1978 he set a new indoor world record for the 1 mile racewalk—6:04. Neal also set new American records for the 1 hour walk—8 miles, 1,021 yards and 25 kilometers—1:15:11, winning those national championships. 1979 showed Pyke to be improving even more. He won the Pan American 20 km trials in a new American record of 1:27:1 and broke that at the Spartakiade in Moscow, U.S.S.R., for 13th place with a time of 1:26:33. In August of '79 he won the National 20 km Championship, beating a really class field.

Neal's training consists mainly of 1–1½ hours racewalking per day during the week and 2–2½ hours on the weekend. He believes in the hard-easy principle of training and recuperation and emphasized to me that most important to him was his one day of rest. He considers that his best workout! Interval work on the track is done only before the really big meets.

From his progress, Neal should be a best bet to make the 1980 Olympic Team. I wish him luck.

would call out to me and wish me luck and say to their friends, "That's the American who walks with Ladany," and "All honors to you, American—stop and drink." I would stop and share some water from a canteen, thank them with the bit of Hebrew I knew, shake hands and wave good-bye only to be welcomed a little father on in that same gracious manner. It was beastly hot, around 95°F but I didn't mind. I was well watered and on a high. So high that I covered 100 kilometers, doing the route twice, and wasn't even tired. I found my group from the language school I was attending and marched with them through Jerusalem to the applause and screams of the tremendous crowds lining the way.

Hopefully, I can get some people marches introduced into this country, so that we all can share the camaraderie and the majestic beauty that we have in this great country of ours.

20

THE JUDGING OF RACEWALKS

Racewalking is the only footrace in athletics where style and legality are strictly supervised. To win in running, all you have to do is get there first. Even to remain in the race, a walker must adhere to the rules of walking. Here again is the IAAF definition of racewalking:

Walking in progression by steps so taken that unbroken contact with the ground is maintained. At each step, the advancing foot of the walker must make contact with the ground before the rear foot leaves the ground. During the period of each step when a foot is on the ground, the leg must be straightened (i.e., not bent at the knee) at least for one moment, and in particular, the supporting leg must be straight in the vertical upright position.

Accordingly, there are clearly two distinct rules that cannot be broken:

1. There must be one foot on the ground at all times.
2. At some point in the stride, the leg must fully straighten in the vertical upright position.

Breaking one or both of these rules will be cause for the athlete's disqualification from the race. Enforcement of the rules is carried out by a chief judge assisted by any number of judges as deemed necessary for the conduct of the race.

New York World-Telegram
Wednesday, August 4, 1948

The first rule, that of keeping one foot on the ground at all times, is quite clear. The heel of the forward-reaching foot must make contact with the ground before the toes of the pushing foot can leave the ground. For if you have both feet off the ground at the same time, you are actually running. But determining whether or not a walker is keeping contact with the ground is nearly impossible. At times, especially at the start or finish of a close race, daylight can clearly be seen under both feet. When it is so flagrant, then an immediate caution is to be issued by the chief judge. The judging of this rule is especially difficult because of the speed of the athlete's steps—sometimes at the rate of three to four steps per second. Infraction of this rule is called *lifting* or *floating;* that is, when it appears there are indications that the athlete is not racewalking. Those indications are:

1. Head bouncing up and down
2. Too high a back kick
3. Landing flat-footed (not illegal but leads to trouble)
4. Arms so vigorous that they appear to pull the athlete off the ground
5. An overall appearance of jogging

These indicators are only that, and cannot or should not be used against the athlete to elicit a caution or a disqualification. Only infractions of the IAAF rule are the basis for caution or disqualification. However, a judge can suggest to a walker that he is in danger of receiving a caution by issuing him a warning and telling him that he is bouncing, or whatever the case may be, and to settle down. Although some feel that it is tantamount to coaching, a judge can give unlimited warnings to a walker who shows signs of lifting or creeping. If, in the opinion of the judge, the athlete has violated a rule, the judge reports to the chief judge who also observes the athlete and, if he concurs, gives the caution. A walker is not entitled to a second caution during a race. The second infraction will bring disqualification.

The other infraction of the IAAF rule is where the leg is not being straightened. It is called *creeping* and is much easier to detect. Observation of this infraction must be made from the side so as to study whether or not the knee is bent constantly, or if the athlete is straightening the leg and then rebending it at the last moment in order to get extra help from the thigh muscles. When there is a question, check the front thigh muscles (quadriceps). They should smooth out when the knee is straightened as the body is passing over the leg. Occasionally, only one leg will manifest this, and the athlete appears to be hopping as well. In either case the infraction is subject to warning, caution or disqualification.

In many cases the race director or coordinator arranges for a well-qualified person whom he knows to be at the race and appoints him as chief judge. Then the chief judge contacts several other judges on his list according to the size, importance and location of the race.

When a local race is held on a track, two or three judges are sufficient. If it is a championship race, it is best to have a total of five; four judges can supervise each quadrant while the chief judge roams. On a road course three judges should be a minimum, with the judges able to move along by bicycle or car or on foot. Again, if it is a long course, the more judges the better.

Each judge should have pencil and paper and 3-inch x 5-inch index cards to write down the name and number of each competitor to whom cautions are given. It is a good idea to note where the infraction occurred and why the caution was given. Judges should wear identifying hats and armbands and be introduced to the walkers by the chief judge at the time when he is giving out his pre-race instructions.

When the actual race begins, the judges should place themselves around the track or along the course so that they may observe the walkers. It is very critical in the beginning of a race to be on the lookout for early *lifting*. With the adrenaline flowing and the excitement of the start, the walker is liable to pay more attention to getting a fast start than to walking legally. A judge, upon seeing signs of an infraction, should immediately render a warning to the walker or walkers in order to settle them down. If he deems it an outright violation, he must communicate this to the chief judge, who will approach the walker, wave a white flag at him, and call out his competitor's number. The chief judge then makes a note of the occurrence on his own card. Many walkers settle down after receiving a warning or a caution and go on to walk a fair race. There are some, however, who will, according to Ron Laird, "ignore any sense of responsibility and sportsmanship and try to get away with bad style when they do not see any judges around."

If, in the opinion of three independent judges, a walker is not walking legally, they can disqualify him or her from the race. This can be done with 1 judge and the chief judge, who does have the authority to make the final decision on whether or not the athlete is walking legally. When a walker is to be disqualified during a race after having received a prior caution, a red flag is waved at the athlete and his competitor's number called out. The flag makes the disqualification visual to the other athletes, officials and spectators. If it occurs on a track, the athlete must step off the track. During a road race, the athlete must remove his competitive number.

Another critical point to watch extra carefully is during the last quarter-mile and especially the last 220 yards. Fatigue may cause problems with contact, and during a really close race, with each walker striving to win, one or both feet may be off the ground. The "220 rule," which stated that if a walker fouled during the last 220 yards of the race, automatic disqualification would follow, has been superseded, and wrongly so according to Bruce MacDonald. "Getting through the race without disqualification should be rewarded only to those who walk the entire race legally, and the last 220 yards should not be overlooked."

I asked Bruce, who was a teammate of mine at New York University and the New York Pioneer Club and a tireless worker for the sport, to sum up his many years of judging experience and present us with some tips on the judging of racewalks.

Requirements for Becoming a Racewalking Judge

1. Good eyesight.
2. No prejudices for or against an athlete, a coach, or a team, a region or a country.
3. No predetermined judgment about an athlete's style, whether good or bad.
4. Not afraid to make a decision regarding an athlete's style.
5. A willingness to judge developmental walks as well as the championship races and tryouts for international teams.

Tips for Judging Racewalks

1. Do not make judgments from the front (as the walker is coming toward you).
2. Do not make judgments from the rear (as the walker is going away from you).
3. Walkers must only be viewed (judged) from the side while they are moving within 25 feet up to and after a spot directly across from you.
4. The distance of the "across" viewing spot should be at least 15 feet and not more than 25 feet.
5. The judge should assume a kneeling, squatting, or even lying down position in order to detect any daylight from lifting or floating. (A

good visual aid is to view just the feet by blocking out the upper body with your hand or the index card.)

Viewing Range

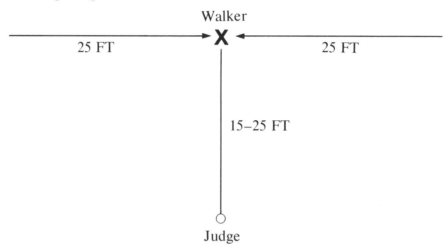

6. A judge should move about from place to place along the course so that the walkers will have to be alert and walk legally at all times.
7. Be especially alert on steep downhills for loss of contact.
8. If the race is on a track, the judge should view only from trackside, not the infield, because grass and curbs block the view.

Each new judge serves an apprenticeship while working with a number of experienced judges. Special judging clinics are conducted from time to time. The role of the racewalking judge is not a very glamorous one and at times quite controversial. But judges are needed and should be respected for their very difficult role of enforcing the rules.

A judge should be decisive and fair with the calls he or she makes. There is no room for poor or timid judging. The highest standards should always be maintained in order for the sport to be looked upon with respect. Racewalkers are quality athletes, and we need quality judges to keep pace with this fast-growing sport.

21

THE HISTORY OF RACEWALKING

Considering the innate competitive nature of man, there probably have been walking races, however informal, since man became bipedal. I'm sure that there had to be some caveman who just had to be home first with the day's kill.

What has been chronicled in the Western world, however, seems to be centered in England, first telling of Sir Robert Carey, who in 1589 walked from London to Berwick, a distance of some 300 miles, winning a rather large wager. King Charles II was well known for his walking ability and was never beaten in his favorite walk from Whitehall to Hampton Court. Would anyone have dared to pass the King?

Early in the 17th century, athletics were an integral part of the fairs and festivals that took place in the towns and villages. The aristocracy employed footmen to run messages or run ahead of the family coach, making arrangements at various inns along the way for meals and lodging. Gentlemen matched their footmen against one another in races and wagered large sums of money. Betting was also prevalent at the fairs and festivals, with the winner getting a handsome share of the prize money. And so, the professional pedestrian was born. But there were then, and there will always be, those who will walk against time and distance just because "they have to."

There are some wonderful stories of the walkers of old, some walking in top hats and knee breeches. They didn't wear athletic garb as we know it today, wearing regular clothes and footgear instead. Occasionally, the rules stated "fair heel and toe," but in long distance events a pedestrian was allowed to trot to ward off cramping of the legs. Some of their exploits were really marvelous, even by today's standards.

In 1762 Mr. John Hague walked 100 miles in 23 hours and 15 minutes.

In 1788 a 55-year-old man, John Batty, walked 700 miles in 14 days.

In 1808 Captain Howe walked 346 miles in 6 days. Two weeks later he raced against Captain Hewetson and won 200 guineas for walking 83 miles in less than 24 hours. This same Captain Howe won a bet that he could cover 60 miles in 12 hours, finishing in 11:50.

Robert Barclay Allardice, also known as Captain Barclay, was one of the better known professional pedestrians. In June of 1801, for a wager of 500 guineas, he arranged to walk 90 miles in 21½ hours. The course was to be on a measured mile between two wooden posts on the road between York and Hull. Scorers were at each end as were

Lank Leonard

lamps during the darkness hours. Resting, refreshing and changing clothes at 16 and at 60 miles, Captain Barclay approached the finish line "strong and hearty" to the cheers of thousands of spectators. He finished the 90 miles in 20 hours and 22 minutes.

When Barclay was 30 years old, he accomplished a feat often attempted but never achieved before—he became the first man to walk 1,000 miles in 1,000 successive hours: 1 mile in each and every hour. The event began at midnight on June 1, 1809, at Newmarket Heath, for a sum of 100,000 guineas. Having no more than half-hour snatches of sleep at a time, Barclay finished his amazing accomplishment at 3:37 P.M. on July 12, 42 days later, to the warm welcome of tumultuous thousands and church bells.

Not to be outdone, a certain Josiah Eaton, in 1815, walked 1,100 miles in 1,100 successive hours. He walked 2,000 miles in 42 days in 1817, later that year walked from Colchester to London in 1 day and

A
Walking Race
1879

Heel-and-toe experts hot foot it around Gilmore's Garden in the "Great International Walking Race." The crowd cheers them on as they sweep by at a gallant 8 miles an hour. The fastest steppers swing along about two-thirds as fast as a good runner or twice as fast as the average walker. They can go on like this for days. They land with a jar on the heel, shift weight quickly to the toe for the next step. Arms pump up and down like pistons to throw the weight forward. But they're disqualified if they break into a run. Some contestants say it's like trying to race forward and pull yourself back at the same time.

From the Bettmann Archive

returned the 51 miles to Colchester the next day. He continued this for 20 successive days for a total of 1,020 miles.

In 1868 the famous American pedestrian Edward Payson Weston completed a walk of 1,326 miles, from Portland, Maine, to Chicago in 26 days. The entire country acclaimed the feat. A march song entitled, "Weston's March to Chicago," was written by a well-known songwriter of the time.

The old Madison Square Garden used to hold 6-day races called, "Go As You Please" races. Weston won many times, walking sometimes as much as 500 miles. In 1879 in the most famous walking race in the world, the Ashley Belt Race in Agricultural Hall, London, Weston walked for 141 hours and 44 minutes and covered 550 miles. In 1907, at the age of 68, he beat his Portland–Chicago record by 29 hours. When he was 75 he walked from New York to Minneapolis to lay the cornerstone for a new athletic club house. He was welcomed to the city by the governor, the mayors of St. Paul and Minneapolis, and the largest crowd ever assembled in the state of Minnesota. For the last 2 years of his life, he was confined to a wheelchair, crippled because of being struck by a taxicab while walking. He died at age 90 in 1929.

Near the turn of the century 6-day races were the craze. These were indoor contests held on 8–16 lap-to-the-mile tracks. The object was to travel as far as possible in 144 hours. Crowds filled New York City's Madison Square Garden in 1879 to watch Charles Rowell, a tiny Englishman, win two of these ultra-distance races and take home $50,000 in prize money. Even though these races were covered extensively in the daily press and the sporting journals of the time, almost no knowledge of them seems to have filtered through to the 1920s.

. . . Then there was this article that appeared in *The New York Times* on May 31, 1910, about the New Jersey couple who walked 40 miles from Woodport to Paterson because the young man's father had asked "every Squire up our way to promise not to marry us." So they kept walking until they found one who would. Love for walking or love for each other—whatever.

During the late 1890s to 1900 and on, more and more leisure time became available to the average working man; an interest in physical fitness took an upswing; and the old competitive urge took hold. For the first time, amateurs took to long distance walking, as opposed to the professionals who found the public's interest waning. Amateurs formed walking clubs and associations. Judging became more strict and the "model walker" was described by the British Race Walking Association as "having a long stride, straight knee, toes well up, complete hip action, upright carriage, vigorous arm swing."

A bit after the turn of the century, specifically the 1908 Olympics held in London, attention was focused on amateur athletics with racewalking receiving high acclaim. The best walker of that Olympics was George Larner, whose style was universally considered to be flawless. He finished first in both the 3,500 meter and 10 mile walks with times still respectable today. He beat representatives of eight countries in each of the two walks.

Testing the stamina of the sturdiest legs in the Metropolitan district: Start!

In early Olympic competition, the racewalking events were dominated by the United States, Great Britain and Canada, until Italy's Ugo Frigerio won both walks in 1920 and one in the 1924 games. Due to protests about judging, the racewalking was dropped from the 1928 Olympics, but a 50 kilometer walk was reinstated in 1932. Thomas Green of Great Britain won that one, but the other European countries began to emerge into prominence. The 10 km walk in the '48 and '52 Olympics was won by Sweden's John Mikaelsson and the 50 km in 1948 by another Swede, John Ljunggren. Ljunggren won a Bronze in 1956 and a Silver in 1960, all in the 50 km racewalk.

The United States, meanwhile, did not have any walkers of top international caliber during the 40s, 50s and up until 1968. The sport was dominated by the Swedes, British, Italians and the Russians.

Then in 1968, when the USA's Larry Young finished third in the 50 km for a Bronze Medal and Rudy Haluza garnered fourth (a dispute evolved about a Mexican finishing second—questionably), the interest and competition in racewalking in America suddenly brightened. Young finished third again in 1972 in Munich, and in the meantime the sport had been gaining tremendously in popularity. Many of our walkers have traveled to Europe to race with various teams and have acquitted themselves rather well in a sport still dominated by the Russians, Germans and now the Mexicans, who have become the best in the world.

As far as competitive racewalking is concerned, I believe that we are just going into our Golden Age. Walkers like Todd Scully, Neal Pyke, Dan O'Connor, Marco Evoniuk, Vincent O'Sullivan, Jim Heiring, Chris Hansen and Dennis Reilly will probably be fighting it out for places on the 1980 Olympic Team, but don't count out guys like Ron Laird, Larry Young and Larry Walker or Dave Romansky. They have a way of getting ready for the big ones. I've probably left out some names of walkers who will have just started about the time this book goes to press. But that's the Olympics for you—in 1948 the world's undeniably best hurdler, Harrison Dillard, stumbled and missed qualifying for the 110 meter high hurdles. So he jumped into another event in which he had never really competed and qualified for the 100 meter dash! He then went on to win the Olympic Gold in that event! Perhaps some smart marathon runners will see the light and switch to racewalking.

22

SOME THOUGHTS FOR THE FUTURE

If you think that we are in the midst of a fitness boom now, just wait. You ain't seen nothin' yet! With the trend toward increased leisure time continuing, more and more people will find and "make" time for their long-neglected bodies. The better informed and assertive people will not sit idly by and allow their future to "happen" to them. They will make their own future. This pertains to matters of health as well. As I have stated earlier, we must look more to ourselves and not rely on doctors to keep us healthy. Pills can cure a specific disease, but no pill can give us instant fitness. Practicing a regular exercise program is like practicing preventive medicine and can ward off the many debilitating diseases brought on by not being fit.

What about those who are not so well informed and not so aggressive in providing for their own health by way of a fitness program? If we want to make life better for ourselves and for our children, then we must do an even better job of educating people with regard to physical fitness, especially in lifetime athletic activities. Those educational efforts should begin in the schools and continue right through to senior citizen groups. As the chapters of the Walkers Club of America have recently encouraged fitness before competition, so should the Road Runners Club deemphasize competition and stress fitness instead. There would be fewer injuries and more pure enjoyment.

Wars are terrible events, but if there is one redeeming feature, it lies with improved knowledge in the field of medicine: injuries and how to treat them to save life and limb. I liken the running boom and its resultant injuries to war and the treatment of injuries. The fields of sportsmedicine in general, and orthopedics, cardiology, podiatry and exercise physiology in particular, have benefited from the boom. Let's do away with all the rivalry among these groups for who is the "supreme guru" or which doctors are more qualified to treat various sports injuries. Instead, let them work together, as teams, and exchange information so that the *athletes* can benefit. After all, isn't that part of the Hippocratic oath: to benefit the injured? All of them should also work in concert to keep the family physician better informed about physical fitness and treating injuries, and set a better example for their patients by not smoking or being overweight. Doctors should realize that they are authority figures on matters of health (both physical and mental) and as such should assume the responsibility for being more assertive about advocating vigorous exercise programs for many of their patients. Remember, a doctor's advice is the single most important motivational tool urging a person to start an exercise program.

We should be glad for more leisure time but be strong about not succumbing to an indolent and sedentary existence. It is so easy to listen to the hucksters cast their spell about this "labor-saving machine" or that "energy-saving device." Cutting up vegetables by hand will use many more muscles in your hands and arms than just pushing buttons. You have to do *some* things with your body, for the less you do, the less you will be able to do.

Develop an attitude about exercise. Be eager to exert energy in some areas, especially when you don't in other areas. You must work your body, and it will work for you.

A shorter working day or a shorter work week will give you more time to walk. I hope that you will walk to work—or at least part of the way. You could walk to the railroad station or the commuter bus stop. You could get off the elevator at the fifth floor and walk the additional five or six flights to your apartment.

I hope that you will make time to racewalk a few times a week.

I wish you the joys and the benefits I've obtained through athletics —and racewalking.